Stedman's Guide to the HIPAA Privacy Rule

Stedman's Guide to the HIPAA Privacy Rule

Kathy Rockel
CMT, FAAMT

LIPPINCOTT WILLIAMS & WILKINS
A **Wolters Kluwer** Company

Philadelphia • Baltimore • New York • London
Buenos Aires • Hong Kong • Sydney • Tokyo

Publisher: Julie K. Stegman
Managing Editor: Lisa Manhart
Development Editor: Robyn Alvarez
Associate Managing Editor: Steve Lichtenstein
Cover Designer: Bot Roda
Interior Designer: Michael Pottman
Typesetter: Maryland Composition, Inc.
Printer & Binder: Quebecor World Book Services

2006

Library of Congress Cataloging-in-Publication Data

Rockel, Kathy.

Stedman's guide to the HIPAA privacy rule / Kathy Rockel.

p. ; cm.

Includes bibliographical references and index.

ISBN 0-7817-6301-0 (alk. paper)

1. United States. Health Insurance Portability and Accountability Act of 1996. 2. Medical transcription—Standards—United States. 3. Medical records—Law and legislation—United States. 4. Medical records—Access control—United States. 5. Privacy, Right of—United States. I. Title.
II. Title: Guide to the HIPAA privacy rule.

[DNLM: 1. United States. Health Insurance Portability and Accountability Act of 1996. 2. Medical Records—legislation & jurisprudence—United States. 3. Confidentiality—legislation & jurisprudence—United States.
WX 33 AA1 R682s 2006]

R728.8.R62 2006

651.5'04261—dc22

2005014724

Foreword

Few people in the medical transcription industry took seriously the early conversations about HIPAA legislation, and those who did found it to be fraught with confusing legal language. What, if anything, would it mean to the medical transcription profession and industry?

One person who studied it from its inception was Kathy Rockel. Kathy took advantage of every available lecture and workshop on the subject of HIPAA, speaking with politicians who influenced the bill and even one of its major authors. She quickly made herself an expert on what HIPAA means to medical transcription, the profession and the industry, writing articles and lecturing to her colleagues, encouraging them to become familiar with how it would impact them.

Now Kathy shares her knowledge with us in this easy-to-read, visually enhanced book. It is all here: a clear explanation of the Privacy Rule, its pertinence to medical transcriptionists, category definitions and compliance requirements for each, implementation dates, and consequences of noncompliance.

The book offers a tremendous service with the inclusion of several sample forms and policies. There are also checklists that are also of great value, offering immeasurable timesaving opportunities for medical transcriptionists and for those who own medical transcription businesses.

Kudos to Kathy and to Stedman's for providing this important book; it should be a must-have for everyone in the medical transcription profession and business.

Pat Forbis, CMT
Pat Forbis & Co.

Acknowledgments

Every book begins with an author who has a dream. And yet, having a dream simply is not enough to make that dream become a reality. What makes the dream a reality is having a publisher who also believes in that dream. For me, that person was Julie Stegman. She took the passion I had about this topic, caught it, believed in it and believed in me, and I am thankful for her vision which allowed my dream to become a reality.

Working with the Stedman's group is always such a pleasure. My thanks to Lisa Manhart, my managing editor, for all of her assistance, encouragement, and constant cheering me on, as well as indulging me on those things I really wanted to see done. I could not have accomplished this without her support. Robyn Alvarez provided development oversight and tremendous assistance to me as a first-time author. I have learned a lot from her as we worked through this journey together. In addition, Jo Cepeda, the development editor for this project, has given me such great feedback to improve this book and make it better for those who read it. Special thanks as well to Yvonne Palmer, the marketing manager, and Chris Kushner, the director of marketing, who did such a great job putting together promotional materials for me, some in very short order, so they could be present for meetings I would attend. Last, but certainly not least in the Stedman's team, are those who served as reviewers for this book. Without their insight and expertise, this book would be a lesser product.

Sharon Allred, CMT
Karen Billingsley
Margaret Collins, MT
Brenda Hurley, CMT, FAAMT
Hope Kremer
Kathleen Kropko, CMT, FAAMT
Elaine Olson, CMT, FAAMT
Barbara Tietsort, MEd.
Patricia Vargo, RHIT

I would like to give a special thank you to two of my mentors in my early days as I began to explore how to put my thoughts and ideas into words on paper for others, Claudia Tessier and Pat Forbis. Both have inspired me as well as been mentors in my development. Claudia's patience in my early days of writing and her willingness to explain suggested edits to my articles allowed me an opportunity to grow immensely and is something for which I will be forever grateful.

I am also thankful and blessed that my employer, Transcription Relief Services, LLC, and its president, Bob Harvey, in particular, have been so encouraging. My coworkers, Regina Rakestraw and Melissa Morris, also have encouraged me and allowed me to bounce ideas around with them, and given some great feedback. They allowed me to share my excitement at seeing this become a reality and celebrated the milestones along the way with me. Thank you.

Last, but certainly not least, I thank Tom Bullock, who has been a constant champion during this process, sharing his ideas, proofing my writing, providing feedback, and believing in my ability to see this to the end. Having that support in my personal life as I spent time on this has meant more than words can express.

Kathy Rockel, CMT, FAAMT

Preface

The legislative arena has always fascinated me. In the late 1990s, we began to hear about HIPAA and how it could impact our industry. Through the efforts of the American Association for Medical Transcription (AAMT), I was fortunate to be involved in responses to the original "Notice of Proposed Rule Making" for the HIPAA Privacy Rule. As the final rule was published and the deadlines for compliance approached, our industry sought solutions to ensure compliance.

Medical transcriptionists have always understood the importance of privacy of healthcare records, and many of the requirements were things we were already doing. I have long had a vision for a simple, easy-to-read text related to the Privacy Rule that would assist medical transcriptionists in showing they indeed are doing all of the required steps to follow the rule. Medical transcriptionists have long requested sample policies, so they did not have to reinvent the wheel. Yet no one was creating this tool. In 2003, a conversation with Julie Stegman from Stedman's led to this vision becoming a reality and the creation of this book.

Within the pages of this book, you will find easy-to-understand explanations of what is required in the Privacy Rule related to medical transcription. It does not matter if you are an employee, an independent contractor, a business owner, or a student of medical transcription. We all have a need to understand these regulations and to be able to apply them in our work settings.

Chapter 1 will give you insight into how a rule is created and what you can do to be sure you remain informed about any changes in the rule in the future. In Chapter 2, we explore the rule in greater detail and give practical application to the work setting of medical transcriptionists, whether an employee, a business owner, or an independent contractor. Chapter 3 provides worksheets to do your own gap analysis within your work setting and determine where you need to make changes in practices and create new policies. It also provides the information that any independent contractor or service owner needs to create his or her own business associate agreement, something required by the Privacy Rule. For me, one of the most exciting things about this book is the sample policies and procedures you will find in Chapter 3. They can be adapted to individual organizations, and electronic copies are provided on the CD included with this book!

The appendices provide you with a variety of helpful resources. Appendix A offers a selection of frequently asked questions (and answers). Appendix B reproduces the checklist for offsite medical transcriptionists created by the 2004 AAMT Legislative Task Force. Appendix C provides a list of industry resources, including websites, mailing addresses, and telephone numbers. Finally, you'll find at the end of the book a glossary of terms, acronyms, and abbreviations.

Medical transcription students will find this volume a valuable addition to their textbooks covering medicolegal issues the industry expects new graduates to know and understand. It gives those students an additional fund of knowledge to apply in their new career.

As our HIPAA hippo takes you through the rule, look for special features throughout the book. You will see icons that will alert you to specific information:

- Nuts and Bolts: This feature provides an outline of what is covered in the chapter.
- Aha!: This feature is meant to give you a deeper understanding of a specific point.
- Caution: This is an alert that asks you to pay special attention to a potential problem area.
- Here's a Hint: This feature offers helpful ways to remember certain key points of the rule.
- The Real World: Case study examples in medical transcription help to show you how the rule applies to real-world situations.
- The Bottom Line: This is a summary of the information covered in each chapter.
- Apply It: Now that you've read through the chapter, apply the knowledge you've learned with these quizzes!

It is my hope that in reading this book you will become a "HIPAAcrat," a term coined by Bill Braithwaite, known in our industry as "Dr. HIPAA" and a primary author of the Privacy Rule. It means one who is enthralled with knowing and learning all he or she can about HIPAA!

Kathy Rockel, CMT, FAAMT

Table of Contents

CHAPTER 1:
Introduction to HIPAA and the Privacy Rule 1

Nuts and Bolts 1
Introduction...1
What Is HIPAA?...2
The Privacy Rule 6
   Terminology...7
   Other Significant Points 12
   Compliance Deadlines..13
   Rule Enforcement...13
The Bottom Line 14
Apply It 15
Answers to Apply It..17

CHAPTER 2:
The Privacy Rule and Medical Transcription 19

Nuts and Bolts..19
Introduction...19
What Does the Privacy Rule Really Do?.......................................20
   What Is Protected Health Information?......................................21
   Who Must Comply and How Does Compliance Impact Work?.....21
   State Laws..22
Applications of the Privacy Rule to Medical Transcription 23
   Policies and Procedures 23
   Training..23
   Use and Disclosure...25
   Minimally Necessary..26
   Access Control..26
   De-identified Information 27
   Confidentiality Agreements 28
   Computer Security 29
   Work Areas...30
   Transfer of Data 30

Destruction of Hard Copy 31
Use of the Fax 31
Use of E-mail 32
Disaster Recovery 33
Offsite Medical Transcriptionists 33
Storage and Retention 33
Audit Trails 35
Termination Procedures 35
Recycling of Computers 36
Access for Educational Purposes 36
Vendors 37
Breaches 38
Complaints 38
Penalties 40
Enforcement 41
HIPAA for the Medical Transcription Service and Independent
Contractor 42
  Are You a Business Associate? 42
The Bottom Line 43
Apply It 45
Answers to Apply It 47

CHAPTER 3:
A Blueprint for Compliance 49
Nuts and Bolts 49
Introduction 49
Where Do I Start? 50
  Gap Analysis Checklist 50
  Vendor Compliance Checklist 53
  Training Checklist 55
What Policies Do I Need? 56
  Privacy Officer Policy 57
    Sample Privacy Officer Policy 57
  Policy for the Use of Protected Health Information 58
    Sample Policy for the Use of Protected Health Information 58
  *Policy for the Use of Protected Health Information in Quality Assurance
  and Educational Programs* 58
    Sample Policy for the Use of Protected Health Information in Quality
    Assurance and Educational Programs 59

Training Policy...59
   Sample Training Policy...60
   Sample Training Policy for Independent Contractors...........................60
Computer Security Policy...60
   Sample Computer Security Policy...61
   Sample Computer Security Policy for Independent Contractors.........63
Policy for Confidentiality Agreements...64
   Sample Policy for Confidentiality Agreements...................................64
Policy for Work Area Arrangements..65
   Sample Policy for Work Area Arrangements in an Office Setting.........65
   Sample Policy for Work Area Arrangements in a Home Office Setting....66
Access Policy for Digital Dictation Systems...67
   Sample Access Policy for Digital Dictation Systems.............................67
Policy for the Use of Hard Copy Protected Health Information.................67
   Sample Policy for the Use of Hard Copy Protected Health
   Information..68
Policy for the Use of the Fax Machine..68
   Sample Policy for Use of the Fax Machine.....................................68
E-Mail Policy...69
   Sample Policy for Use of E-Mail for Employees.....................................70
   Sample Policy for Use of E-Mail for Independent Contractors...........71
Disaster Recovery Policy...71
   Sample Disaster Recovery Policy for Covered Entities and Medical
   Transcription Services...72
   Sample Disaster Recovery Policy for Independent Contractors...........72
Policy for Offsite Medical Transcriptionists...73
   Sample Policy for Offsite Medical Transcriptionists.............................73
Termination Policy...76
   Sample Termination Policy for Employees.....................................76
   Sample Termination Policy for Independent Contractors...................76
Breaches and Sanctions Policies...77
   Sample Breaches and Sanctions Policies for a Covered Entity.............78
   Sample Breaches and Sanctions Policies for a Business Associate......78
Complaint Policy...79
   Sample Complaint Policy...79
Vendor Policy..80
   Sample Vendor Policy for Covered Entities.....................................80
   Sample Vendor Policy for Transcription Service Companies and
   Independent Contractors...80

Policies for Business Associates 81
  Sample Policy for Business Associates...81
  Sample Contracts and Agreements 82
    Sample Business Associate Agreement 83
    Sample of Privacy Rule Language Added to a Transcription Services
    Contract..88
  Policy for Subcontractors...92
    Sample Policy for Subcontractors...93
  Offshore Transcription Policy..93
  A Word About Disclosures 93
  What About Indemnification?..94
The Bottom Line 95
Apply It 96
Answers to Apply It...102

APPENDIX A:
Frequently Asked Questions....................................105

APPENDIX B:
AAMT Paper on Special Considerations for Offsite
Medical Transcriptionists...111

APPENDIX C:
Industry Resources 117

GLOSSARY

Introduction to HIPAA and the Privacy Rule

In this chapter, you will learn:

1. How rules related to HIPAA legislation are created.
2. How the Privacy Rule fits into HIPAA legislation.
3. Key terms in the Privacy Rule.
4. Significant points of the Privacy Rule.
5. Compliance dates for the Privacy Rule.

INTRODUCTION

April 14, 2003, was the "go-live" or compliance date of the HIPAA Privacy Rule. When I visited healthcare providers after that date, I noticed each handled the paperwork differently. Some gave the patient a four- or five-page document to read and sign. Others asked for a signature on a one-page form that said the **Notice of Privacy Practices** had been received. After I read each of the documents given to me, I would say, "I'd like a copy of your Notice of Privacy Practices, please." Were they surprised! Had they not expected anyone to actually ask? Oops! I could see what they were thinking: HIPAA is really here.

If you visited your physician after April 14, 2003, you, too, were probably given papers related to the Privacy Rule. If you are a medical transcriptionist, perhaps your first notice of the rule came as a special training session arranged for you by your employer. Medical transcription students may have seen HIPAA for the first time when it was added to the curriculum. A transcription service company may have received new contracts from clients. They had to quickly make sure the contracts used terms that were covered by the rule and included conditions to which they could adhere.

The entire medical transcription industry scrambled to prepare for the Privacy Rule's compliance date. Where could we go to find the information we needed in terms we could easily understand? What should we do about the liability insurance our customers now required us to carry? What policies and procedures should we create? Where could we find examples that we could adapt to fit our needs? And how in the world would we find time to sleep?

This book is meant to help answer your questions. To begin, Chapter 1 offers a brief overview of HIPAA, explains how the Privacy Rule fits into that law, and lists some very important terms you need to know.

WHAT IS HIPAA?

The letters **HIPAA** stand for Health Insurance Portability and Accountability Act of 1996. As the name suggests, it is meant to make sure people can take their health insurance with them when they move from one job to another.

The drafting of the HIPAA legislation began in 1993. At about the same time, a study was done by the Workgroup for Electronic Data Interchange (WEDI). It showed that the healthcare industry could save billions of dollars if it would record transactions electronically. Later, the huge savings predicted by the WEDI study became the primary benefit of the HIPAA legislation.

Many of WEDI's cost-saving ideas are spelled out in

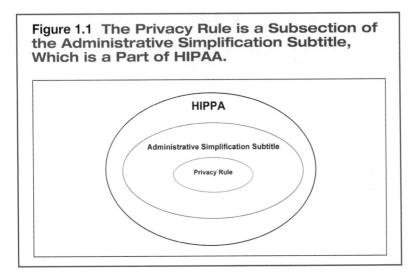

Figure 1.1 The Privacy Rule is a Subsection of the Administrative Simplification Subtitle, Which is a Part of HIPAA.

the rules of the Administrative Simplification provisions of the law (see Figure 1.1). Each of those rules includes standards that help to improve electronic healthcare transactions. A good example of this is insurance billing. Before Administrative Simplification, a patient who had both Medicare and supplemental insurance had to have Medicare billed first. Once Medicare responded, the supplemental insurance company would then be billed. In addition, both had their own formats for how to submit bills, which required many hours to complete. With the new Administrative Simplification rules, the same bill would be sent to Medicare. It would then process the bill and send it on to the supplemental insurance company. Best of all, all the paperwork could be done in the same format.

Imagine having all billing formats standardized! That has been a dream in the medical transcription world for a long time. Standardizing could allow the same claim to be processed much faster, with fewer people. It also could provide reimbursement to the physician faster. All of this adds up to money saved.

The major rules of the Administrative Simplification part of HIPAA address topics such as development and implementation costs, timely testing and updating procedures, and adaptability to changes in infrastructure. The major rules are:

- *The Transactions and Code Sets Rule.* Insurance billing is similar to medical transcription in a service setting. That is, each

The Real World

Often, when someone refers to HIPAA, he or she may in fact be talking about the Privacy Rule. Keep in mind that the Privacy Rule is only one part of HIPAA.

insurance company uses its own forms in its own unique format. Those who are doing the billing must do it differently for every insurance company with which they interact. This rule is meant to standardize those transactions, so that the process is easier, more efficient, and cost effective.

- *The Privacy Rule.* The subject of this book, the Privacy Rule addresses the concerns people have about how their health information is used and stored.

- *The Security Rule.* This rule aims to make sure computer systems used in health care are accessible only to those who have a valid need to know. For example, it addresses the use of passwords to sign on and off computers. It explains how information transmitted electronically is encrypted. And it tells how servers and computers should be housed.

- *The National Identifier Rule.* This rule addresses unique identifiers for healthcare providers and employers. Still in development are standards for enforcement and health-plan identifiers, which at this time have no projected publication date.

- *The Enforcement Rule.* When this rule is ready, it will describe how all HIPAA rules are to be enforced. It will describe the penalties that may used when someone is in violation. It also will include procedures for both criminal and civil penalties.

Aha!

The Process of Creating Rules

1. The Department of Health and Human Services (DHHS) publishes notice of a proposed rule in the *Federal Register*. The public has 60 days to comment.

2. DHHS responds to each comment by either making changes in the proposed rule or not.

3. The final rule is reviewed by DHHS and others who are affected by it.

4. If Congress approves after 60 days of its own review, the final rule is published.

5. Sixty days after that, the rule becomes effective.

6. Entities who are impacted by the rule have two years and two months in which to become totally compliant.

The process for a rule to become effective is a long one. HIPAA's Privacy Rule was no exception. In 2000, the Privacy Rule was made available to the public for comment. As a result, the Department of Health and Human Services (DHHS) received over 50,000 responses. Each one on average included three different topics of concern—a total of over 150,000 comments. People were clearly worried about the privacy of their health information.

Whew! I'm glad this book is just about the Privacy Rule.

DHHS also sought comment on the workability of the rule in the complex healthcare industry. The department wanted to make certain that there were no unanticipated consequences that might harm patients. So the industry was given one more month to comment.

In its final form, the Privacy Rule became effective April 14, 2001. There currently exists no other federal legislation that guarantees a patient the right to privacy of his or her health information.

Stay abreast of any changes in the rules. Watch for notices of proposed rule making, and determine if compliance will impact your work setting. Notices can be tracked through the *Federal Register* as they are

Aha!

The HIPAA Privacy Rule Timeline

1999 Congress misses the deadline to pass legislation on protecting the privacy of health information. So the Privacy Rule is drafted by the Department of Health and Human Services (DHHS) and offered for public comment.

2000 The final Privacy Rule is published. The effective date is extended to 2001 in order to give Congress time to review it.

2001 Congress okays the Privacy Rule and re-publishes it for comment by the healthcare industry. One month later, it becomes effective.

2003 Effective date of compliance is April 14, 2003.

published. You can find a link to the *Federal Register* in the resources section of the appendices.

THE PRIVACY RULE

Why should you as a medical transcriptionist care about the HIPAA Privacy Rule? Whether you are an independent contractor, a service owner, an educator, or a student, consider this scenario:

> ///// **CAUTION** /////
>
> The Privacy Rule may be reviewed and modified on an annual basis. Stay up to date with changes to be sure you remain compliant.

After examining a patient, a physician in *California* dictated his findings to a service in *Virginia*. The service used a medical transcriptionist who lives in *Florida.* She in turn relied on a quality assurance editor who is in *Minnesota*. Quite sometime later, the patient found out that the privacy of her medical records had been breached. Who could she turn to for help?

Do you know? Which of the four states involved, if any, do you think would have jurisdiction? Before the HIPAA Privacy Rule, there was no answer to this question. There was no federal law or rule that covered all states. HIPAA now offers a way to provide privacy for a patient's information in any state. Though it has not yet been tested in a court case, it is speculated that the state that would have jurisdiction in the scenario above is the one in which the patient resides.

Here's a Hint

"Is it HIPAA or HIPPO, and why should I care?" The answer is HIPAA—the Health Insurance Portability and Accountability Act of 1996—and you should care because it impacts YOU.

Again, why should you care? Because HIPAA impacts everyone working in the healthcare industry, including medical transcriptionists. Even you. Perhaps most important of all, a reason to care is that the Privacy Rule helps to ensure quality patient care. Always aim to maintain the integrity of the system, so that patients willingly give information to their healthcare providers, knowing that it will be protected.

Terminology

Trying to understand all of the terms in the Privacy Rule can be daunting. But learning just the important ones can help you figure out how the rule applies to your own work setting. Those terms are defined and discussed in the following paragraphs. The first one is:

- **Covered entities**—one of the two distinct healthcare groups identified in the Privacy Rule. (The other group is called *business associates*.) A covered entity may be a health plan. It may be a healthcare provider, such as a hospital or a physician. It also may be a healthcare clearinghouse. (A good definition for each of these covered entities is offered a bit later in this chapter.)

A medical transcriptionist is *never* a covered entity. If you work as an independent contractor, you are *not* a covered entity. If you are an employee of a medical transcription service, you are *not* a covered entity. If you are an employee of a hospital or a physician's office, you are a part of the "workforce" of a covered entity, but you are not the covered entity.

The next term for you to learn is *business associate*. Medical transcriptionists are often considered business associates.

- **Business associate**—an individual who is not part of the workforce of a covered entity but who performs a function for the covered entity that involves protected health information. Examples include medical transcription companies and coding firms.

A medical transcriptionist who works as independent contractor may be a business associate, depending on who his or her

> If you are an independent medical transcriptionist who works directly for a covered entity, you are a business associate.

client is. That is, if you are self-employed (an independent contractor) and your client is a covered entity, you are a business associate. Lawyers, accounting firms, and consultants may also be business associates.

You are *not* a business associate if you are a self-employed medical transcriptionist and your client is a transcription service company. In that case, you would be a *subcontractor*. The transcription service would be the business associate of its client, the covered entity.

There are times when a covered entity is a business associate. For example, when a hospital transcription department provides

Table 1.1 Medical Transcriptionist Roles and Contracts.			
If you are a(n)...	**Then your role is...**	**And you will need a...**	**Will the Privacy Rule apply?**
Employee of a hospital or a physician and work either at home or in the office	Employee (workforce) of a covered entity	Normal confidentiality agreement for employees	YES
Medical transcription service	Business associate	Contract for services and a business associate agreement	YES
Employee of a medical transcription service	Employee of a business associate	Normal confidentiality agreement for employees	YES
Independent contractor who has a contract with physician offices and/or hospital	Business associate	Contract for services and a business associate agreement	YES
Independent contractor who has a contract with a medical transcription service	Subcontractor	Subcontractor agreement	YES

services to doctors, the doctor is the covered entity, and the hospital is his or her business associate.

Look at Table 1.1. It shows what roles a medical transcriptionist has in a variety of work settings. It also shows what contracts are necessary for each of those roles.

More important terms from the Privacy Rule are defined below:

- **Protected health information (PHI)**—information about a patient's past, present, or future medical treatment that contains data that can reasonably identify the patient. Health information that has had all patient identifiers removed (that is, it has been **de-identified**) is *not* protected health information.

- **Health plan**—an insurance company or any program or plan that provides for payment of the cost of health care. Note that the government-funded health plans which are specifically listed in the Privacy Rule are considered covered entities.

- **Health-care clearinghouse**—a covered entity that processes protected health information for others. For example, a clearinghouse that provides billing services will take information that is in a non-standard format or language and convert it to an acceptable standardized one. Medical transcription does *not* fit in this category.

- **Healthcare provider**—a physician or healthcare facility, both of which are covered entities. For them, all patient information is protected by the Privacy Rule, whether it is transmitted orally, electronically, or as a handwritten document. Note that the physician or healthcare facility is the covered entity, not the employees who work there. Employees—whether they work in the healthcare provider's office or from home—are considered a part of the "workforce."

- **Health care**—services or supplies related to the health of an individual. Health care includes:
  - Preventive, diagnostic, therapeutic, rehabilitative, maintenance, or palliative care.
  - Any counseling, service, assessment, or procedure related to either the physical or mental condition or functional status of an individual.
  - Any prescription drugs or prescribed devices, equipment, or other items.
- **Health information**—any information related to someone's past, present, or future mental or physical health, no matter what form it is created or received in. It also is information that relates to past, present, or future payment for the health care of an individual. The Privacy Rule protects all health information that can reasonably identify the patient.
- **Standard**—a condition or requirement that describes specific criteria for products, systems, services, or practices related to the privacy of health information. Criteria may include classification of components; specifications of materials, performance, or operations; or step-by-step procedures.
- **Standard-setting organization (SSO)** or standard development organization (SDO)—an organization accredited by the American National Standards Institute (ANSI) that develops and maintains standards for information transactions and data elements. One example of an SSO is an organization you are probably familiar with—the American Society for Testing and Materials (ASTM).
- **Use**—sharing health information within an entity, which requires no authorization from the patient. An example of "use" would be transcribing a physician's recorded report for a patient's healthcare record.
- **Disclosure**—sharing information outside the covered entity's control, which requires authorization from the patient. An example of "disclosure" would be sending a patient's information to a pharmaceutical company for marketing purposes.
- **Business associate agreement (BAA)**—a contract that outlines the duties and responsibilities of a business associate in dealings with a covered entity, using the specific language outlined in the Privacy Rule. Any medical transcriptionist in the role of a

business associate must have one of these contracts with his or her client.

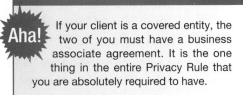

If your client is a covered entity, the two of you must have a business associate agreement. It is the one thing in the entire Privacy Rule that you are absolutely required to have.

- **Workforce**—employees and paid or unpaid volunteers, trainees, and other personnel whose conduct in the performance of work for a covered entity is under the direct control of that entity. If you are a medical transcriptionist who is an employee of a hospital or physician's office, you are a part of the workforce of that hospital or office. Independent contractors are not considered part of a workforce.

- **Independent contractor**—in medical transcription, this is a self-employed person who provides medical transcription services to others. This person is *not* an employee of the clients he or she serves. However, he or she might be a business associate (has contracted directly with a covered entity), or he or she might be a subcontractor (see the definition below).

The terms that follow are not part of the HIPAA Privacy Rule, but they are important to your business:

- **Subcontractor**—this is a medical transcriptionist who works as an independent contractor for a business associate. This transcriptionist does not have a contract with a covered entity. Instead, he or she has been hired by a service or by another independent contractor who actually has a contract with the client.

- **Confidentiality agreement**—a document that should be signed by all medical transcriptionists, whether an employee, independent contractor, or medical transcription service. It says that you will protect the confidential nature of the records you work with and will not divulge them to anyone who should not have access to them. If you are an independent contractor, this agreement may already be a part of your client contracts.

- **Contract for services**—a written agreement between someone who needs medical transcription service and someone who will provide it. It outlines how the relationship works, such as how payment will be made, and lists the specifics about the work to be done. It is an agreement that a business associate should have with all contractors. However, it is not a "business associate agreement" and should not be confused with one.

> ///// **CAUTION** /////
>
> The Privacy Rule outlines penalties for noncompliance, some of which include large fines and possible prison time.

Other Significant Points

The Privacy Rule gives patients specific rights in regard to their health information. For example, a patient has the right to inspect and receive copies of his or her records and to request amendments or changes. However, there are exceptions. One such exception has to do with psychiatric records. They do not have to be given to the patient if the provider feels they could cause the patient harm. When this is the case, the provider must give a reason for not allowing the patient to see the information.

Note that it is the covered entity, not the business associate or subcontractor, who is responsible for providing records to a patient. Make sure your business associate contracts spell that out. This will help you avoid dealing directly with patients should they become aware that you have access to their information.

Another point to keep in mind is that the Privacy Rule does not apply to a business associate. It applies only to the covered entity. Here is where it gets a bit tricky. When a covered entity gives a business associate protected health information, any breach in the privacy of that information is the covered entity's responsibility. Listen closely now. As a result, many covered entities require business associates to have liability insurance, so that any fees or fines related to a breach may be collected.

One final point to remember is that the Privacy Rule spells out the requirements for training in all matters related to protecting the privacy of health records. Covered entities must make sure their employees get that training. To prove it, they must describe all of their policies and procedures in writing. They also must document their training sessions.

You will learn more about these last three points in the following chapters.

Don't be like Alice's rabbit—late, late for a very important date.

Compliance Deadlines

The deadline for compliance with the Privacy Rule was April 14, 2003. This means all covered entities, such as a hospital or physician's office, should now have their own compliance plan in place and active. I hope with this "nuts and bolts" guide you, too, will be compliant—whether your role is as a student, subcontractor, business associate, or employee of a covered entity.

Rule Enforcement

Several government agencies are involved in the enforcement of the Privacy Rule. The **Secretary** of the Department of Health and Human Services (DHHS) has the right to delegate responsibility for monitoring compliance and accepting complaints. So, that responsibility is with the Office of Civil Rights (OCR), a branch of DHHS. OCR is responsible for all *civil* complaints and for impos-

The Real World

April 14, 2003, was the compliance deadline for all covered entities, except small health plans. They had an additional year to comply.

ing any fines related to violations of the Privacy Rule. The U.S. Department of Justice is responsible for investigating any *criminal* complaints related to the Privacy Rule and is empowered to prosecute offenders. For all other HIPAA rules, the Centers for Medicare and Medicaid Services (CMS) will be responsible for monitoring and investigating violations as well as imposing fines.

THE BOTTOM LINE

The Privacy Rule and HIPAA

- The Privacy Rule is one of four rules in the Administrative Simplification Subsection of the HIPAA legislation.

Main Groups Addressed by the Privacy Rule

- *Covered entities*—health plans, healthcare clearinghouses, and healthcare providers. Medical transcriptionists who work as employees of these groups are a part of the workforce and will follow policies developed by their employer.

- Business associates—those who perform a function for a covered entity that requires access to protected health information. Medical transcriptionists who are transcription service owners or independent contractors providing services directly to a covered entity are business associates.

Rights Recognized by the Privacy Rule

- The rule protects the privacy of health information.
- It also allows patients access to their health information.

Apply It

Multiple-choice questions are offered here to help you test your understanding. Answers are provided on page 17.

1. The primary benefit of the Administrative Simplification Subsection of HIPAA is to:
   a. save billions of dollars in health care.
   b. protect the privacy of health information.
   c. outline a patient's rights to health information.
   d. protect covered entities and business associates.

2. Sarah provides volunteer services at the local hospital. According to the Privacy Rule, her position fits into which one of the categories listed below?
   a. covered entity
   b. business associate
   c. workforce
   d. healthcare provider

3. Dan is a medical transcriptionist who works as an independent contractor for a one-physician office. Does Dan need a business associate agreement with the physician?
   a. Yes, because Dan is part of the physician's workforce.
   b. Yes, because Dan is a self-employed transcriptionist.
   c. No, because the physician is not a covered entity.
   d. No, because the physician has a small practice.

4. Gabrielle is a medical transcriptionist who is an employee of Memorial Hospital. Her position fits into which one of the categories listed below?
   a. independent contractor
   b. business associate
   c. subcontractor
   d. workforce

5. The deadline for compliance with the Privacy Rule was in:
    a. 1996.
    b. 2001.
    c. 2002.
    d. 2003.

Answers to Apply It

1. a. The Privacy Rule protects health information. However, the Administrative Simplification Subsection was created in response to the WEDI study that showed billions of dollars in savings in health care.

2. c. The definition of "workforce" includes volunteers.

3. b. Dan is a medical transcriptionist who is an independent contractor—a self-employed person who contracts directly with a covered entity. So Dan must have a business associate agreement with the physician. Note that Dan's client, the physician, is a covered entity, no matter what the size of his or her practice.

4. d. Medical transcriptionists who are employees—not independent contractors—of a hospital or physician's office are a part of the workforce.

5. d. April 14, 2003, was the deadline for compliance with the Privacy Rule.

2 The Privacy Rule and Medical Transcription

In this chapter, you will learn:

1. The application of the Privacy Rule in medical transcription.
2. Which policies and procedures you should write for your organization.
3. What makes information "de-identified."
4. How to be sure your work area meets the requirements for the Privacy Rule.
5. The activities necessary for a secure computer system.
6. Special requirements for the medical transcription service or independent contractor.

INTRODUCTION

In September 2004, it was announced that former President Bill Clinton would have heart bypass surgery at a New York hospital. Imagine how hospital personnel must have felt knowing the former president would be under their care. Imagine as well how hectic it must have been as the Secret Service descended on the facility to perform its routine security tasks. What if you were the medical transcriptionist who worked on the president's preoperative history? Or the transcriptionist who transcribed his operative note?

One day after his discharge from the hospital, the *New York Daily News* reported breaches in the privacy of the president's medical records. According to the paper, "Columbia Presbyterian Hospital suspended a total of 17 workers, including a doctor, several supervisors, a lab technician, and a number of clerical employees for trying to access the top-secret computer records." Though the newspaper story did not include a confirmation of this news, it did note that the hospital has a "zero-tolerance policy" on protecting patient privacy. And the policy extends to their most senior staff. Sources were reported to say that workers were caught after they used their passwords to look at the records. It was also reported that a janitor was offered $1,000 for his hospital ID. In all likelihood, the information they tried to access was on documents prepared by medical transcriptionists.

Enter the HIPAA Privacy Rule with all of its forces. Now, in addition to hospital policy, individuals—even former presidents—are protected by federal rules and regulations that come into play to provide protection for patient information.

◉ WHAT DOES THE PRIVACY RULE REALLY DO?

The Privacy Rule was created for one very simple reason—to protect the privacy of the patient's health information in every situation. It gives patients specific rights to access their information. It also includes civil and criminal penalties for those who violate its protections.

Protect the patient's health information. That's the key.

The Privacy Rule:

- Gives patients more control over their health information.

- Sets boundaries on the use and release of health records.

- Establishes appropriate safeguards that healthcare providers and others must put in place.

- Holds violators accountable with civil and criminal penalties that can be imposed if they breach a patient's privacy rights.

- Helps to strike a balance between what must be kept private and what may be disclosed (to protect public health, for example).

- Offers patients an opportunity to make informed choices based on how protected health information may be used by healthcare providers and others.
- Enables patients to find out how their health information may be and has been used.
- Limits the release of information.
- Gives patients the right to examine, obtain a copy, and request corrections to their own health records.
- Empowers patients to control certain uses and disclosures of their health information.

What Is Protected Health Information?

Protected health information, or PHI, is health information containing data that can reasonably identify the patient. It is related to a patient's past, present, or future mental or physical health. It is created or received by a healthcare provider, public health authority, employer, life insurer, school or university, or healthcare clearinghouse. It also is information that relates to past, present or future payment for health care. It includes such things as a patient's name, address, social security number, telephone number, occupation, age, diagnoses, physical examinations, and treatment plans.

Who Must Comply and How Does Compliance Impact Work?

Technically, the Privacy Rule applies only to covered entities. However, in order to safeguard themselves, covered entities may ask business associates to comply with the law in the same way they do. For example, in a transcription service that has 16 clients, maybe five of them will ask the owner to show how he or she has implemented the Privacy Rule.

Medical transcriptionists work in a variety of settings—an office in a hospital or clinic, an office in a medical transcription service, even a home office. They may be employees of a medical facility or transcription service. Or they may be independent contractors, offering their services to whom they please. Compliance with the Privacy Rule will be the same or very similar for each setting. The specifics will come into play after you evaluate your situation and determine whether or not you are a business associate. (See Chapter 1 on how to decide if you are one.)

The Privacy Rule also requires "reasonable" safeguards to ensure the privacy of a patient's information. Keep in mind that any setting where you transcribe records will be affected by the rule. Then, as you work toward compliance, continue to ask yourself this question: "Would this effort be considered a reasonable one?"

State Laws

If a state law gives a patient more protection than the Privacy Rule, the state law must be followed. This is called **state preemption**. So, as you can see, you must be able to understand the state laws where you work.

Do you remember the situation in which a patient and her doctor are in one state and the transcription of her records is performed in another? (Refer back to Chapter 1.) The question it asked was which state would have jurisdiction over a breach of privacy, the state in which the patient received care or the state in which the transcriptionist works. We will have a definitive answer when a lawsuit is filed and a court is asked to interpret how the Privacy Rule should be applied. Until then, all we know is that best business practices would follow the law of the state in which the patient received care.

Here's a Hint

The Health Privacy Project, which is included in the resources section of the appendices, has provided a link on their website where you can investigate what each state's laws may say about HIPAA.

///// **CAUTION** /////

Pay attention to the Privacy Rule *and* be keenly aware of related state laws as well. Why both? Because Privacy Rule definitions clearly suggest that medical transcription companies are business associates. But that may *not* be true in every state. In the state of Texas, for example, they are considered covered entities—and covered entities are held responsible for much more than a business associate is. So it is critical that you learn what your state's laws say. And remember: State law, if it provides more protection, overrides federal rules.

APPLICATIONS OF THE PRIVACY RULE IN MEDICAL TRANSCRIPTION

Whether you are a hospital or clinic employee, an employee of a medical transcription service, or an independent contractor who has your own accounts, all medical transcriptionists have to show compliance to the Privacy Rule. It applies to every setting.

Policies and Procedures

Compliance with the Privacy Rule begins with the development of your own policies and procedures. They will be the basis for how you will handle a variety of situations. If you are an employer, your policies must be developed before your staff gets Privacy Rule training.

Whether you are a medical transcription service or an independent contractor, you need written policies. They can demonstrate your intent to comply with the rule. They also serve as a line of defense should you ever be involved in an audit for compliance. For example, if your clients are being audited, they may ask you to verify that you have been trained to meet Privacy Rule standards. If you are an employer, they may ask you to prove that all of your employees and subcontractors have been trained, too. So be prepared. Be ready to supply a copy of your policies and procedures related to the rule. And document any training related to HIPAA.

(Chapter 3 will address specific policies and procedures as well as provide samples.)

Training

The Privacy Rule requires that all covered entities provide training to their workforce about the rule. There are two aspects required of training: training new employees and retraining current ones. (Keep in mind that the word "workforce" includes employees,

Aha! If you are a medical transcriptionist who contracts directly with covered entities and business associates, you should have your own written policies and procedures, even if you are a one-person business.

volunteers, trainees, and other people whose conduct is under the control of the covered entity.) Training also extends to management staff and boards of directors.

Training by a covered entity is based on a person's role in the organization. For example, it is not necessary to train the janitorial staff to fax protected health information. That is not what they do. In contrast, it is necessary to train all medical transcriptionists in the workforce because they handle protected health information every day.

Medical transcription service companies should also train their employees. If you own a service company, document the training you provide. You might include a description of each training session and the topics covered; the date, time, and place of the session; the name, title, and experience of the trainer; and the names and positions of the employees who attend. Keep a copy of the documentation in your personnel files.

Independent contractors should document the training they receive on their own as well. If you are an independent contractor, keep records. A certificate of attendance, an official course or seminar description, session handouts, and a copy of the check you used for payment will do.

Topics to be covered in training for compliance with the Privacy Rule include:

- Definition of protected health information.
- State laws.
- Use and disclosure of medical information.
- Minimally necessary information required to perform a job.
- Access control to computer systems.
- Password protection for computer systems.
- Confidentiality agreement requirements.
- Computer security policies.
- Work area policies.
- How to handle transport of data.
- How to protect physical media.
- Policies for the destruction of protected health information.
- Policies for the use of the fax.

- E-mail policies related to protected health information.
- Storage and retention of protected health information.
- How to deal with breaches of protected health information.
- How the complaint process works.
- Penalties for violations of the Privacy Rule.
- The role of the **Office of Civil Rights** in enforcement.

   If you are ever asked about Privacy Rule training—whether as a result of an audit or to assure a new client, you should be able to prove that you have been trained.

Use and Disclosure

In general, health information may *not* be used or disclosed unless authorized by the patient or allowed by the Privacy Rule. For instance, a healthcare provider may not sell a patient's information to a pharmaceutical company's marketing department unless the patient has given him or her permission to do so. Note that some health information may be disclosed without a patient's consent, if it is for the purpose of treatment, payment, or **healthcare operations**, as long as the privacy of that information is protected.

Here's a Hint

Training of the workforce is required at two different times:
- *When someone joins the workforce.*
- *Any time a policy change impacts a person in his or her role in the workforce.*

   Medical transcription falls into the category of *healthcare operations.* These are the activities required to conduct the business of a covered entity. That is, a patient does not have to give his or her consent for a covered entity to give information to a medical transcriptionist. But it is important that the information is used only for its intended purpose.

   In the early days of the Privacy Rule, people wondered if it would stop the use of offshore transcription companies. This is not the case. The rule does *not*

Aha! A medical transcriptionist does *not* need to get a patient's permission to access medical records. The Privacy Rule allows access. If the records are to be used only in activities required to conduct the business of a covered entity (such as a hospital or physician), no permission is needed.

give a patient the right to say where his or her records are transcribed. That decision is left solely to the covered entity. Patients may request that their records not be sent offshore, but the healthcare provider is not required to comply with this request.

Minimally Necessary Information

The Privacy Rule states that when information is to be released, it must be kept to the least possible amount of information needed to do a job. That is what the term *minimally necessary* means.

For medical transcriptionists, minimally necessary information includes all of the medical records that need to be transcribed. It also includes data such as the patient's name, medical record number, date of admission, date of discharge, and so on. That data is needed to make sure transcribed reports can be properly identified. In addition, there are times when it is important to access information within the medical record to ensure an accurate report. For example, it is very helpful to be able to look at lab values to determine if a dictation is correct.

Access Control

The Privacy Rule requires *access control* or control over who can access protected health information in any form. Whether you work from home or in a hospital transcription department, you

The **Real World**

It was early on a Monday morning. The patient was in his hospital room, waiting to be taken to surgery when in through the door popped one of his previous medical transcription students. "Just checking to see how you're doing," she said. The former student was now a clerk in the transcription department of the hospital and was charting the day's medical reports. She noticed her instructor's name, read the report, learned he was having surgery, and decided to stop in to give him her "best wishes."

Fortunately for all concerned, this incident occurred pre-HIPAA. While the clerk did require access to medical information to perform her job, the way she used the information was completely inappropriate. In today's world, she would be in violation of the Privacy Rule.

must control who has access to the information you need to do your job. Access should be based solely on the need to know. For example, a medical transcriptionist or a quality assurance editor may need access to an entire medical record in order to verify information. In contrast, a supervisor may need access only to a limited amount of information.

No! You may not use my computer to play Internet games.

All computer systems should be set up with unique identifiers and passwords. For example, if you use a dictation system that lets you listen to a report before it is transcribed, a unique identifier should be used for access to that system. Your password should not be shared with others. It should be used only to access a system for work related to your job. If you have employees, they should be held accountable for the use of their passwords. If you are an independent contractor working from home, steps should be taken so that no one else in your household has access to the patient information on your computer.

De-Identified Information

The Privacy Rule allows for sharing of de-identified information. Since such records can no longer identify the patient, they are not considered protected health information. The rule lists 18 items that must be removed in order for information to be labeled "de-identified." Those items are:

- Names.
- All geographic subdivisions smaller than a state (except for the first three digits of the zip code in some cases).
- All elements of dates (except year) for dates directly related to an individual (e.g., birth date, admission date, discharge date, date of death); all ages over age 89; and dates indicative of that age.
- Telephone numbers.

Don't leave anything to chance. Be careful when you de-identify.

- Fax numbers.
- E-mail addresses.
- Social Security Numbers.
- Medical record numbers.
- Health plan beneficiary numbers.
- Account numbers.
- Certificate/license numbers.
- Vehicle identifiers and serial numbers, including license plate numbers.
- Device identifiers and serial numbers.
- Web Universal Resource Locators (URLs).
- Internet Protocol (IP) addresses.
- Biometric identifiers, including finger and voice prints.
- Full-face photographs and any comparable images.
- Any other unique identifying number, characteristic, or code.

The AAMT Book of Style for Medical Transcription advises against using identifying information in the body of a medical report. The **American Association for Medical Transcription (AAMT)** further advises that such information should be located only in the demographics section of a report. That way, it may be readily deleted. Transcriptionists should adopt this practice. But beware: physicians often dictate identifying information in the body of a report. So, when there is a need to de-identify, read the report carefully, and delete *all* potentially identifying data.

Confidentiality Agreements

All medical transcriptionists should sign a confidentiality agreement.

//// **CAUTION** ////

You can delete patient demographics from the heading of a report. You can even replace the patient's name with the words "the patient." Neither action de-identifies a report. You also must eliminate all potentially identifying data. That includes such information as a pacemaker's unique model and serial numbers. Be alert. Read a report carefully before labeling it "de-identified."

It states that the information you access will not be shared with anyone unless necessary to perform your duties. Expect it also to say that any violation of confidentiality will lead to disciplinary action, up to and including termination. Though not required by the Privacy Rule, it is a good idea to update these agreements annually. (A sample confidentiality agreement is included in Chapter 3.)

Computer Security

In order to protect health information, computers and digital dictation systems must be secure. Do this with unique identifiers and passwords that are required to log onto a system. People with access to protected health information through a computer or digital dictation system must understand that they are not allowed to share their passwords with anyone. They will be held responsible for any activity conducted under their passwords. Covered entities should make it mandatory that access is never shared.

Passwords should periodically expire and be reset. Master password lists, if they are kept, should be held in a locked storage area where only those who have a need to know have access (the information systems [IS] manager, for example).

Computer monitors should not be placed in areas where the public can see them. To prevent viewing of health information by any unauthorized person, screen savers should be set to go on after only a few minutes of inactivity. If it becomes necessary for medical transcriptionists to leave their work stations, to take a break, or to have a meal, they should log off the system before leaving their work stations. They can log on again when they return.

Aha!

Computer Security Checklist

- Systems have unique identifiers and passwords that periodically expire and must be reset.
- There is no sharing of passwords.
- The master password list is kept in a locked area with access only by those who have a need to know (such as IS managers).
- Screen savers are set to activate after short periods of inactivity.
- Users log off the computers when they leave their work stations.
- Computer screens face away from public areas.
- Anti-virus software is installed and routinely updated.
- Operating systems are updated as recommended by manufacturers.
- Spyware software is installed.
- A computer that has file sharing is never used for protected health information.

It's best to keep passwords secure.

Anti-virus programs should be installed in all computers. The programs are always to be kept up to date. Perform operating system updates as recommended by the manufacturer. Also, consider anti-spyware software to ensure file security. In addition, no programs that allow file sharing, such as music programs or games, should be installed on a computer that houses protected health information.

Though this book focuses on the Privacy Rule, keep in mind that there is also a Security Rule. It defines the technical requirements for ensuring the security of computer systems.

Work Areas

In hospital settings, medical transcriptionists are often a part of the health-information management department. Often, they are located in the middle of the work space. Their computers are shared among staff members who work different shifts. To protect access and passwords, it is very important that one staff member signs out of the system before another one signs on.

A work area where medical transcription is performed must be secure. It should be located away from high traffic areas, so health information will not be exposed to passersby. Computer screens should face away from doors and windows. Safeguards should be in place to prevent voice files from being overheard. When medical transcriptionists help each other to decipher a difficult word, voice files should be played through a headset, not over a speaker. When not occupied, the work space should be locked.

Transfer of Data

Ideally, a physician dictates a report in a private spot, not in the middle of a busy patient-care area. Once the report is recorded, the voice files are sent for transcription. They are either accessed by the transcriptionists, who can dial directly into the dictation system, or they are sent to the transcriptionists at their work sites. The electronic transfer of voice files must be done in a secure manner. No one but the person to whom they are routed should be able to access those files.

In some cases, medical transcription is still done on cassette tapes. These tapes must be transferred in a secure manner and stored in a locked area when not in use. If tapes are physically transported, they should be in a locked box for transport. If tapes are shipped, they should be addressed to a specific person, who is required to sign for them upon receipt.

Text files should be encrypted when they are transferred electronically unless the transcriptionist is working directly on the covered entity's system. The transcriptionist may print the files. He or she may deliver them to the provider by hand in a locked box. Files may also be transferred with a direct PC-to-PC connection, which should be set up with unique identifiers and passwords.

Destruction of Hard Copy

Medical transcriptionists often work with copies of patient schedules or hospital census sheets. These documents are to be shredded after use. If information is provided in an electronic file, it should be deleted from the computer when the dictation for that period of time is completed. Any copies of information that are used for the processing of transcribed reports should be treated in the same manner.

It is possible that the clerical support staff may have copies of a census, a surgery schedule, or a to-be-admitted list. These documents should never be left out in the open where passersby can read them. When they are no longer necessary to perform the duties of the job, they should be shredded.

Use of the Fax

Providers often ask to have transcribed documents faxed. This may include faxing to another hospital to which the patient is being transferred, to a specialist who will be seeing the patient, or to a nursing home where the patient is being admitted. The Privacy

Whenever I get a tough dictator, I shred. Relieves all my frustrations.

Rule does *not* prohibit the use of a fax to send health information. However, fax machines used to send protected health information should be located in a private area, not a public one. Where possible, fax machines that transmit or receive protected health information are not to be used for general office faxing. This helps to avoid accidentally attaching health information to a routine fax.

Always send a cover sheet with any faxed health information. It should include a statement that identifies the document as private and confidential. It should explain that the fax is meant only for the eyes of the addressee. Finally, it should ask for the sender to be notified if the wrong person receives the fax. (A sample cover sheet is provided in Chapter 3.) When you find out that an unintended recipient received your fax, make sure that the fax is either returned or destroyed. Document the incorrect transmission and the steps taken to make certain this does not occur in the future.

When sending a fax, be sure that the recipient is aware that it is on the way. This lets him or her retrieve it immediately. Faxed documents should never be left in a fax tray. Be sure there are designated personnel who are assigned to retrieve and process faxed information as soon as it arrives. Ask for a fax transmittal confirmation, and save it for future verification.

It is also important to use preprogrammed fax numbers. They will help you to avoid misdialing a number. If numbers cannot be preprogrammed, always verify the number before sending a document.

Use of E-Mail

More and more often e-mail is being used for protected health information. Though encryption is not required by the Privacy Rule, the Security Rule does recommend it. So, if you are e-mailing patient files to your clients or patient schedules to your transcription providers, make sure the information is encrypted. It makes good business sense to do so. All e-mail communication that includes protected health information should also include a privacy statement similar to the one described for a fax.

Disaster Recovery

Because technology is not failsafe, you need a disaster recovery plan. The Security Rule requires it. Computer and digital dictation systems should have automatic backups in place. Backups should be stored where they are secure but accessible, should a system need to be rebuilt. Data may be backed up daily onto a tape system for retrieval if a disaster should occur. Software applications that have an automatic setting should be set to back up data every two to five minutes.

> ///// **CAUTION** /////
>
> What if a major hurricane blows through your area, knocking out all power and access to electronically stored information? What if lightning were to destroy the hard drive of your dictation system? Backup of all systems would be critical in both of these instances. Only by having the appropriate backup systems in place can you make sure information is protected and able to be restored.

You will have to review the final Security Rule for all disaster recovery requirements.

Offsite Medical Transcriptionists

The transcription industry as a whole increasingly uses offsite medical transcriptionists. They may be employees of hospitals or physician offices, independent contractors, or employees of a medical transcription service. Special consideration must be taken in each setting to ensure protection of health information. The 2004 AAMT Legislative Task Force created a checklist to be used with offsite medical transcriptionists. It is reproduced in the appendices of this book with permission of both AAMT and its authors.

Storage and Retention

How do you store information? For what period of time? The Privacy Rule requires that protected health information be kept for a period of six years. Once information is transmitted to the patient

The **Real World**

An acquaintance told me that she was surprised to receive a follow-up call from the hospital emergency department where she had recently been treated. The call was to inform her that her HIV test had been completed, and because of the results, she would now require additional testing. To her knowledge, no such test was performed during her visit to the hospital.

Upon investigation, it was discovered that a medical transcriptionist, working from home, had left hospital census sheets lying on her desk. Believing it would be fun to play a joke, her teenager telephoned the patients with the HIV story. In light of today's Privacy Rule, this could be construed as using information for "malicious harm." It is a criminal offense punishable by not more than a $250,000 fine, not more than 10 years in prison, or both.

Remember: *All* hard copy information must be shredded when it is no longer needed in order to protect the information it contains.

record, no protected health information should be stored on an individual computer. If you are an offsite medical transcriptionist, return work immediately upon completion. No copy should be stored on your hard drive. When protected health information is retained until receipt is acknowledged and payment is received, then it should be removed from the computer, transferred to a removable storage medium (CD, for example), and stored securely in a fireproof locked cabinet or receptacle. After payment is received, the media should be appropriately destroyed. Work logs should be handled in the same manner.

When cassette tapes are used for transcription, they should be placed in a locked storage area, if no one is in the immediate area to monitor their access. They should be erased as soon as the dictation has been

At the end of each day, make sure all information is secure.

processed and before reuse. Digital dictation systems should be programmed to archive voice files when they are no longer needed. In addition, when staff leaves for the day, all records with patient information on them should either be shredded or locked in a secure area. This will prevent others, such as cleaning personnel, from having access.

(Retention of transcribed documents and voice files by business associates will be addressed in the business associate section.)

Audit Trails

The Privacy Rule gives patients the right to an accounting of all disclosures of their medical information. In order for a covered entity to comply with this requirement, audit trails must be kept. (An audit trail is a list of all disclosures of an individual's information.) It should be noted here that audit trails do not apply directly to medical transcription. A covered entity is not required to disclose to the patient where his or her medical records are to be transcribed.

Covered entities and business associates alike would be wise to include how they will handle disclosures in their contracts. The contract language should say the business associate is not allowed to make any disclosures except to the covered entity. This helps the covered entity maintain control. It also helps in the documentation of the audit trail should information be requested by the patient. If you do not choose to have a clause like this in your contracts, it is possible that you would find patients coming to your office, asking for record inspections, changes, and copies. To avoid this, agree to make disclosures only to the covered entity or to your client.

Termination Procedures

Any employee may be fired or resign. When a medical transcriptionist is no longer employed, certain procedures must be in place to remove all access to any health information. Keys to the facility and to its work spaces must be

Here's a Hint

When a medical transcriptionist has been terminated, it is vital to let everyone know he or she is:

G – Get

O – Out

N – Notice to

E – Everyone who needs to know!

surrendered. User names and passwords must be removed from systems. All other access must be removed as well, including access to company e-mail systems. Each of these steps should be included in a written policy and documented to show that they have occurred.

Recycling of Computers

Computers are often recycled in health care. They are donated to schools or moved from one employee to another. It is very important to note that simply deleting files from a computer does not remove everything from memory. Hard drives must be reformatted when a computer is recycled. This ensures that all protected health information has been removed and is no longer accessible to others. It also ensures that an otherwise philanthropic gesture does not turn into a situation where penalties are imposed because of a breach of a patient's privacy.

Access for Educational Purposes

Medical transcriptionists are often trained on "live" dictation or by viewing previously transcribed documents. This training method may be used for a transcriptionist who is new to an account or for a student in an internship program. It also may be used for the purpose of providing quality assurance feedback to medical transcriptionists.

When discussions first began about the Privacy Rule, everyone wondered if the rule would prohibit the use of protected health information for training. The answer is now posted on the Frequently Asked Questions page of the Office of Civil Rights website. It says:

> The definition of healthcare operations in the Privacy Rule provides for conducting training programs in which students, trainees, or practitioners in areas of health care learn under supervision to practice or improve their skills as healthcare providers. Covered entities can shape their policies and procedures for minimum necessary uses and disclosures to permit medical trainees access to medical information, including entire medical records.

This official response allows medical transcriptionists and medical transcription students to access protected health information during training sessions. Be sure to have a written policy on training. It should say that trainees will be given access to only the minimum information necessary and will not disclose the information they access.

Vendors

Vendors are often used for various functions within the medical transcription arena. One example are vendors who sell software. One of them might install the product. Another might provide on-site training. The local computer whiz, who works on a system when it develops problems, may be considered a vendor as well. In some cases, an employment agency that seeks out medical transcriptionists for open positions is a vendor. Another example might be a company that does billing for a medical facility or a medical transcription service. If you are renting office space and have a cleaning service, remember it is also considered a vendor.

What special rules apply to these vendors? The functions of each vendor must be evaluated to determine how the rule applies. For example, if a software vendor has access to protected health information, a covered entity is required to enter into a business associate agreement with him. However, if the vendor simply sells the software but has no access to protected health information, then he would not be considered a business associate.

One medical transcription service routinely processes delivery to its customers using PC-to-PC connection software. Following one transmission, they received a call from a client. He told them that he had received reports belonging to another facility. Prior to the Privacy Rule, this was, at best, a mistake. The service would apologize for it and then take precautions to ensure that it would not happen again. In all likelihood, the facility that was originally supposed to receive the files never knew a breach occurred. But enter the Privacy Rule and that all changes.

When a business associate breaches protected information, the Privacy Rule requires him or her to notify the covered entity. The covered entity must then receive reasonable assurances from the business associate that steps have been taken to prevent this error from happening again.

Breaches

All breaches of privacy should be documented. So should the steps taken to ensure a breach will not occur again. In addition, policies related to sanctions against individuals who breach the information must be in place. Responsible for enforcement of the Privacy Rule, the Office of Civil Rights indicates on its website that they handle investigations of complaints. If a complaint generates an investigation, it would be critical for a facility to be able to show that the breach has already been identified and addressed.

It also is a good idea to have levels of sanctions for the workforce. For example, if a breach was truly a simple mistake, perhaps a warning should be issued. But if the information was breached with malicious intent, for personal gain, or with the intent of using and/or selling it, then immediate dismissal would be appropriate. Keep in mind that sanctions are applied by an employer or covered entity. You could still be faced with civil and criminal penalties if the breach ends up in the hands of the government.

Complaints

Covered entities are required to have complaint procedures in place for possible breaches of privacy. The first step in filing a complaint is to contact the **privacy officer**. If you are an employee of a hospital or physician's office, their privacy officer is the person to contact. Medical transcription services will have a person designated for this role as well. An independent contractor may serve as the privacy officer for his or her own business. Medical transcriptionists should be aware of who the privacy officer is at their facility and how to contact him or her.

Sure it's rough to get complaints, but NO retaliation is allowed!

If you own a transcription service and have had a breach within your company, your privacy officer must immediately report the breach to your client. If you are an independent contractor providing services to a medical transcription service, you would report a breach to the company with whom you have a contract. It is their responsibility to report it directly to their client.

In any case and with any breach, documentation is extremely important. Only by documenting what you have done to handle a breach and how you have made changes to be sure it will not happen again can you show that you made a good faith effort to correct any problems.

Addressing complaints should start within the facility itself. An option is for a formal complaint to be filed with the Office of Civil Rights, which will then investigate the complaint. Complaints to the Office of Civil Rights may be submitted either on paper or electronically. They also must be submitted within 180 days of the time the person filing the complaint knew or should have known about the breach. It is possible that such a complaint will trigger an audit of the covered entity. So it is critical for the breach to be documented, as well as steps taken to ensure it does not occur again.

A covered entity has a responsibility to mitigate any damages as a result of a privacy breach. This would include steps to remedy any harm caused by the breach.

The Privacy Rule also includes a "no retaliation" requirement. This means that no retaliation can be taken against a person who files a complaint, as long as the person has a good-faith belief that the practice is unlawful, the manner of opposition is reasonable,

Civil Penalties

- Not more than $100 for each violation of a particular standard, with the total amount of all violations of the identical amount not to exceed $25,000 per year.

Criminal Penalties

- Basic violation—a fine of up to $50,000 and not more than one year in prison, or both.

- False pretenses—a fine of up to $100,000 and not more than five years in prison, or both.

- Intent to sell, transfer, or use for commercial gain, or malicious harm—a fine of up to $250,000 and not more than 10 years in prison, or both.

and the person's actions do not disclose protected health information in violation of the Privacy Rule. This requirement extends not only to patients, but also to members of the workforce of a covered entity.

Penalties

Severe penalties, both civil and criminal, may be imposed for violations of the Privacy Rule. *Civil penalties* include fines of not more than $100 for each violation of a particular standard, with the total amount of all violations of the identical type not exceeding $25,000 per year.[1]

There are exceptions to civil penalties. There may be no civil penalty for a violation that is caused by someone who does not know he or she has violated the Privacy Rule and, even after exercising due diligence, would not have known about it. However, the failure to comply must have a "reasonable cause" (such as a fax accidentally being sent to a wrong number), was not willful intent, *and* action to prevent the same violation from occurring again was taken within 30 days of learning about the failure.

For example, if you accidentally send a patient report to the wrong physician, this would be "reasonable cause" and not "willful intent." Action must be taken on this to show how you can make sure the same thing will not happen again, and that action must be taken within 30 days of knowing about the mistake. If you are investigated for this breach and can show you have done all this, civil penalties may not apply. So it is clearly beneficial to address any complaints or possible violations in a timely manner.

---

[1] Civil penalties are addressed in the notice of proposed rule making for the enforcement rule issued by the Department of Health and Human Services in April 2005.

Note that civil money penalties apply only to covered entities. They do not apply to business associates of the covered entity.

In addition to civil penalties, there may be *criminal penalties* for violations of the Privacy Rule. They apply to violations that are committed knowingly. They include:

- A fine of not more than $50,000 and imprisonment of not more than one year, or both. These may be imposed for a simple breach (if you intentionally fax patient information to the wrong provider, for example).

- If the offense is committed under false pretenses, the person may be fined not more than $100,000 and imprisoned for not more than five years, or both. An example of this is claiming the release of information is to allow for proper patient care when the person receiving the information has no right to it at all.

- Finally, if the offense is committed with the intent to sell, transfer, or use the information for commercial gain, personal gain, or malicious harm, the violator may be fined not more than $250,000 and imprisoned for not more than 10 years, or both. This example would include someone who sold a celebrity's information to a tabloid newspaper.

Understand these penalties. They have severe implications for anyone who violates the standards. All training efforts should include information about the penalties and the serious nature of privacy violations.

Enforcement

Enforcement of the Privacy Rule has been assigned to the Department of Health and Human Services (DHHS). Enforcement for all

Here's a Hint

HIPAA rules will be enforced as follows:

- *For the Privacy Rule, civil penalties are enforced by the Office of Civil Rights. Criminal penalties are enforced by the Department of Justice.*
- *For all other HIPAA rules, enforcement is the responsibility of the CMS.*

other rules has been assigned to the **Centers for Medicare and Medicaid Services (CMS)**. Both organizations have indicated on their websites that they intend to provide technical assistance for compliance issues and seek voluntary compliance where possible. Within the Privacy Rule, civil penalties are addressed and administered by the DHHS. Criminal penalties, however, will be enforced by the Department of Justice.

HIPAA FOR THE MEDICAL TRANSCRIPTION SERVICE AND INDEPENDENT CONTRACTOR

Medical transcription is often performed by way of an agreement, either with a medical transcription service or an independent contractor. Independent contractors are, in fact, business owners, even if the business consists of one person. Thus, independent contractors are subject to the same provisions of the Privacy Rule as any medical transcription service company.

Are You a Business Associate?

///// **CAUTION** /////

An independent contractor might make the mistake of thinking that because he or she is a one-person business, and not a medical transcription service with employees and contractors, the Privacy Rule does not apply to him or her. Don't get stuck in this way of thinking! In the future, that mistake could cost you clients and business.

Whether or not a business associate relationship exists is determined solely on the function performed, not on who the person or entity is. It is possible that an organization could be a covered entity in one situation and a business associate in another. If a business or individual is performing work for a covered entity, has access to protected health information in order to perform that service, and is *not* a part of the covered entity's workforce, that person is most likely a business associate. Examples of business associates:

- A medical transcriptionist who works as an independent contractor for a hospital or physician's office.

- A medical transcription service that provides medical transcription services to hospitals and physician offices.

- A hospital transcription department that provides medical transcription services to the physician offices in the local area.

Note: The Privacy Rule holds that only a covered entity is responsible for compliance. At the same time, most clients expect that their business associates will have policies and procedures in place to ensure compliance. Instituting the policies and procedures described in this book would be a good show of faith on the part of a business associate.

THE BOTTOM LINE

General Requirements

- Each business associate is required to enter into a business associate contract, or agreement, with the covered entity. This is the one requirement for business associates in the rule. (The specific requirements of this agreement will be discussed in Chapter 3.)

- Clients may use e-mail as a means of communicating with their business associates. If this includes protected health information, such as patient schedules, census sheets, and so on, it is important that this information be protected. The Privacy Rule does not require encryption. But keep in mind that it does say you must make reasonable efforts to protect the information. Encryption could be identified as one of those reasonable steps.

- Data transfers should always be done in a secure manner. Often small businesses or independent contractors do not have information systems personnel to investigate the best way to handle this. The good news is there are software programs available that can assist. An application service provider (ASP) could help to provide the security needed. There also are companies that offer security services for small businesses or independent contractors.

- When addressing storage and retention, it is recommended that protected health information be kept by a business associate only as long as necessary to facilitate processing of the dictation, verification of delivery, and billing. This concept is supported by an ASTM publication *Standard Specification for Management of the Confidentiality and Security of Dictation, Transcription, and Transcribed Health Records, E1902.*

- The business associate agreement should indicate the business associate will make no disclosures of protected health information other than to the covered entity and for only that which is necessary to conduct their business. Inserting this language helps a small business or independent contractor from being required to make disclosures to patients. In essence, a transcribed document is not a final report until the physician authenticates it. Thus, disclosure to the patient or anyone else would not be appropriate. Not only does this relieve the business associate of this responsibility, it also allows the covered entity to remain in control of tracking disclosures for audit trails.

- If a business associate uses subcontractors who have access to protected health information, the business associate must make sure those subcontractors agree to protect that information. The best way to be sure this is covered is to address it in your subcontractor's written agreement. Keep in mind that the subcontractor may be a medical transcriptionist. Other possible subcontractors may include a billing service, if it is given access to the actual transcribed reports or any patient information, perhaps for billing verification.

- You can determine if a business associate agreement or subcontractor agreement is required by identifying what function the person serves and whether or not the person has access to protected health information. The attorney for a hospital or physician's office may or may not be a business associate. If the attorney is defending malpractice suits and has access to protected health information, he or she would be a business associate. An attorney who performs contract review, for a service, an independent contractor, or a hospital or physician's office, would not have access to protected health information and therefore would not be a business associate. An accounting service that provides billing for a medical transcription service and has to access the transcribed documents to verify volumes to bill would be a subcontractor to that business; it would not be a business associate because the relationship is not directly with the covered entity. Each situation must be evaluated separately to make an accurate determination about what kind of documentation is required to remain compliant.

Apply It

Multiple-choice questions are offered here to help you test your understanding. Answers are provided on page 47.

1. If you have employees, when should you train them on the Privacy Rule?
   a. when someone joins the workforce
   b. when changes in policies impact a person's role
   c. annually
   d. a and b only

2. Which one of the following must be removed for the report to be considered "de-identified" under the HIPAA Privacy Rule?
   a. photographs from the patient's gallbladder surgery
   b. the patient's high school graduation date, which was 40 years ago
   c. the serial and model numbers for the patient's intraocular lens implant
   d. All of the above

3. As a medical transcriptionist, which of the steps below should you take to be sure your computer is secure?
   a. Periodically expire and reset passwords.
   b. Assign a unique identifier to each user.
   c. Install anti-virus software.
   d. All of the above.

4. When asking a coworker for help in understanding a difficult dictation, the recording should NOT be played over a speaker. In light of the Privacy Rule, the reason is:
   a. the speakers muffle the sound quality.
   b. doing so gives others access to protected health information.
   c. using speakers distracts others in the adjacent work areas.
   d. All of the above.

5. The Privacy Rule prohibits the use of a fax to send protected health information EXCEPT in emergency situations.
    a. True
    b. False

6. When assigning a computer from one employee to another employee at the same facility, it is NOT necessary to remove protected health information since both employees are part of the same workforce.
    a. True
    b. False

7. Medical transcription students can no longer work with "live" dictation because the Privacy Rule prohibits this practice.
    a. True
    b. False

8. As a result of a medical transcriptionist filing a complaint about a possible privacy breach, which one of the following could occur?
    a. disciplinary action of the transcriptionist for disclosing protected health information in the complaint
    b. reassignment of the transcriptionist to a job with no access to protected health information
    c. an investigation initiated by the Office of Civil Rights
    d. All of the above

Answers to Apply It

1. d. The Privacy Rule does not require annual training although annual refresher courses would be beneficial.

2. c. Answer "a" is not a full-face photograph, and answer "b" would make a patient's age approximately 57–60, which is not over 89.

3. d. All of the possible answers listed are included in the list required to ensure computer security.

4. b. While answers "a" and "b" may indeed be true, they have nothing to do with the Privacy Rule.

5. b. False. The use of a fax to send health information is permitted as long as it is done with appropriate safeguards to protect the information.

6. b. False. The second employee would have no need to see the information on the computer, so all protected health information should be removed before the computer is recycled.

7. b. False. It is acceptable according to the Privacy Rule to use protected health information in the education of healthcare workers.

8. c. False. The rule specifically prohibits any retaliation against someone who files a complaint.

3 A Blueprint for Compliance

 **Nuts** & **Bolts**

It's all about compliance! In this chapter, you will learn:

1. How to perform a gap analysis to measure compliance efforts.
2. How to decide what policies you will need.
3. How to create a policy for your business or yourself.
4. What sample policies look like, so you can use them in your work setting.
5. What a business associate agreement should look like.

INTRODUCTION

The Privacy Rule has now been in effect since 2003. Everyone should be compliant, right? Take a walk back in time with me. I recall the early days of the "HIPAA-is-coming" mantra, when many felt as if Chicken Little had entered the world of medical transcription. "Who will enforce all of these rules?" was the question. The answer: "The industry will police itself." However, since medical transcriptionists have always understood the notions of confidentiality and privacy and since ours has often been considered a "hidden" profession, some of us believed it would be highly unlikely for the government to knock on our doors. Flash forward to today. As you will see in this chapter, there have been discussions about medical transcription in newspapers, in legislators' offices, and even on the news. That increased awareness no longer allows medical transcriptionists to not be proactive in their approach to HIPAA regulations.

● WHERE DO I START?

It's easy to zap the gaps once you identify them.

By filling out checklists similar to the ones described below, you can gather all of the information you need to make sure you are compliant with the Privacy Rule. They will help you get organized. And they will help you find out where you need to create or change your own policies and procedures. As you identify areas that need to be addressed, consider assigning a primary person to be responsible for each task. If you are an independent contractor, consider adding deadlines for each item as a way to help you keep on track.

Gap Analysis Checklist

Medical transcriptionists have discovered that the best approach to ensuring compliance to the Privacy Rule is to start with a *gap analysis*. A gap analysis will quickly show which requirements are already in place and which are not. While the term *gap analysis* may sound a bit intimidating, it really is only a matter of making a list (Figure 3.1). The list is made up of the items the Privacy Rule requires or what you need to have in place for compliance. Once that's done, you can compare it to what you currently have. That process will identify the gaps and help you create an action plan to eliminate the gaps.

As a medical transcriptionist, you are probably quite familiar with this process. For example, consider this scenario: In order to meet your goals for the day, you must transcribe 1,500 lines of dictation. This is "what you need." It is noon, and you find you have transcribed 1,000 lines so far (what you currently have). By comparing what you need to what you currently have, you

Figure 3.1 Example of a "Gap Analysis Checklist."

Medical Transcription Gap Analysis Checklist				
Item	Yes	Need	Responsible Party	Deadline
1. Is a Privacy Officer (or the responsibilities of a Privacy Officer) assigned?				
2. Do you know your state's laws and how they relate to the Privacy Rule?				
3. Do you have a policy for how protected health information is used in each role?				
4. Is there a Privacy Rule training process in place for your current workforce? If you are an independent contractor, do you have a mechanism to obtain training? If you use independent contractors, do you have documentation that shows they have had the proper training?				
5. Is there a training process in place for new additions to the workforce? If you are an independent contractor and have subcontractors, do you make sure they have had training?				
6. For covered entities and medical transcription services, do you have a process that allows for additional training when changes in policy impact a person's role?				
7. For covered entities and medical transcription services, have all staff members been trained on the Privacy Rule as it applies to their roles?				
8. Do you have a mechanism in place to document training?				
9. Do you have policies that define how disclosures are made?				
10. Is there a policy stating that only the minimum necessary protected health information to do the job will be disclosed?				
11. Do your computer systems have access control built into them, so that access to protected health information is role-based?				
12. Do all computer systems require a unique identifier for access?				
13. Do all computer systems require passwords that periodically expire and must be reset?				
14. Do all medical transcriptionists sign a confidentiality agreement? If you are an independent contractor, do you have a confidentiality agreement with all of your clients?				
15. Are confidentiality agreements updated annually?				

Figure 3.1 *Continued*

16. Do computer security policies outline steps to ensure the protection of a patient's health information?				
17. Do all computer systems have anti-virus programs that are updated regularly?				
18. Are there policies that outline how a patient's health information should be protected within the transcription work area?				
19. If protected health information is transferred electronically, are the transfers secure?				
20. Is all hard copy of protected health information destroyed by shredding upon completion of its use?				
21. Are fax machines in a secure environment?				
22. Do fax cover sheets have a confidentiality statement on them?				
23. Do you have a policy on how faxes are sent, so that protected health information is secure?				
24. Do you have a disaster recovery plan?				
25. Are there specific guidelines written for offsite medical transcriptionists?				
26. Do you have termination policies that immediately remove a person's access to all protected health information?				
27. With offsite medical transcriptionists, do you have a policy for appropriately returning or destroying all protected health information?				
28. Do you evaluate all contracts and establish which require a business associate agreement and which may require sub-contractor agreements?				
29. Is the appropriate agreement developed with those who require it?				
30. Do you have policies that ensure protected health information is removed from a computer before that computer is recycled?				
31. Do you have a business associate agreement or subcontractor agreement, as appropriate, with each vendor who accesses protected health information in the course of providing services for you?				
32. Do you have a specific procedure that allows for someone to file a complaint about a potential breach in privacy?				
33. Do your complaint policies include a "no-retaliation" clause?				
34. Do you have clearly defined sanctions for anyone in the workforce who violates privacy policies?				

know you have 500 more lines to produce. You have identified the gap. You can then put into place a plan to allocate time and resources for transcribing those additional 500 lines by the deadline. Thus, you have eliminated the gap. The process of ensuring you have done all of the necessary steps for the Privacy Rule is no different.

It's easy to zap the gaps once you identify them. The process of a gap analysis involves:

1. Identifying where you need to be.
2. Identifying where you are.
3. Identifying the gaps.
4. Implementing a plan to zap the gaps.

Vendor Compliance Checklist

Another good tool to help you verify compliance with the Privacy Rule is a vendor compliance checklist. It can help you identify all of your potential business associates, what protected information they access, and what agreements you will need to have with them. You can use a checklist like the one shown in Figure 3.2. If you are a transcription manager in a hospital, use a checklist like the one shown here to find out if you need business associate agreements with your vendors. If you are a transcription service company or independent contractor, you can determine your own status as well as that of your subcontractors. If you are an independent contractor who works as a subcontractor, you will see from the checklist that you need to have a subcontractor agreement in place.

Here's a Hint

When determining if someone is a business associate or not, be sure you consider:

1. *Services provided by the contractor.*

2. *Whether or not the contractor has access to protected health information and, if so, what protected health information?*

3. *How protected health information is accessed.*

4. *Date of current contract, oral or written.*

5. *Whether or not a business associate agreement is needed and, if one exists, date signed.*

6. *Date the business associate agreement ends.*

Figure 3.2 Example of a "Vendor Compliance Checklist."

Vendor Compliance Checklist						
Vendor	Protected Health Information Accessed	Methods	Business Associate Agreement Needed?	Subcontractor Agreement Needed?	Sign Date	Privacy Rule Agreement End Date
ABC Transcription Service (medical transcription service or independent contractor, providing services to hospitals)	Dictated patient reports, patient census	Digital dictation system; files delivered via FTP site	Yes, with clients	Yes, for independent contractors	1/1/05	1/1/06
Sue Smith, CMT (individual medical transcriptionist, providing services to a physician's office)	Dictated visit notes	Daily tapes via courier; reports returned via courier	Yes, with the physician's office	Yes, when any of the work is contracted to another independent contractor	2/2/05	2/2/06
Speedy Courier Service	Dictated tapes; transcribed medical reports	Delivered in secure locked box	No, because the box is locked and therefore no access to protected health information	Yes	1/1/05	1/1/06
Office Systems, Inc.	Dictation system, dictated reports	Service contractor for digital dictation system	Yes, if you are a covered entity	Yes, if you are a business associate or subcontractor	1/1/05	1/1/06
Computers, Inc.	Protected health information stored on hard drives, tapes, and other back up systems	Routine maintenance of computer systems and installation of new software	Yes, if you are a covered entity	Yes, if you are a business associate or subcontractor	1/1/05	1/1/06
XYZ Billing Systems	Patient files used by transcription service for line counting and billing	Billing company for transcription service	No, because you do not have a contract directly with the covered entity and are a subcontractor	Yes	1/1/05	1/1/06
J. D. Smith, Attorney	None	Business issues only attorney	No	No		
J. R. Jones, Attorney	Potential access to patient files	Malpractice attorney	Yes, for covered entities only	No	1/1/05	1/1/06
T & S Cleaning Service	None	Office clearing; no protected health information in open areas	No	No		

Figure 3.3 Example of a Training Session's Proof-of-Attendance Certificate.

Piedmont Triad Chapter of AAMT

VERIFICATION OF ATTENDANCE AND CREDIT

This document is verification that

ROBYN ALVAREZ

attended the Spring Workshop of the Piedmont Triad Chapter of AAMT on

MARCH 25, 2005

and received the following credits:

___√___ HIPAA and Medical Transcription

1 MEDICOLEGAL CREDIT

___√___ Medicolegal Aspects of Confidentiality

1 MEDICOLEGAL CREDIT

APRIL 3, 2005   *JANICE NOWAKOWSKI*

Date   Continuing Education Chair

Training Checklist

All training should be documented. If you are an independent contractor, you will want to be sure you document the training you receive. In addition, if you use subcontractors, you will want to ask them for proof of their training. That might be an attendance certificate (Figure 3.3) and/or an official seminar description and payment receipt. For employees, documentation should include the em-

Figure 3.4 Example of a Training Verification Sheet.

Training Verification Sheet		
Employee Name		
Date of Training		
Training Officer		
Subjects Covered	New	Policy Change
Protected Health Information		
Minimum Necessary		
Patient Rights		

ployee's name, date of training, the subjects covered, and whether the training was for a new policy or related to a change in policy. Records should be kept for each employee and placed in his or her personnel file. A sample form for documenting employee training is shown in Figure 3.4.

I need a checklist, so I know I won't miss a thing.

WHAT POLICIES DO I NEED?

Compliance becomes relatively painless when you have a solid set of policies and procedures. These serve as your guide to ensuring that you are doing what is required by the rule. In addition, policies serve as your documentation should you have a breach. They show what the expectation was and how breaches are handled. When questions arise, having a policy moves you closer to finding easy solutions.

It is important to note that *the Privacy Rule only applies to covered entities.* A medical transcription service company and independent contractors are not required to have the policies suggested in this chapter. But aren't your clients covered entities or business associates? They will expect you to do everything necessary to be able to show compliance if they are audited. A wise business person will put these policies in place even though they are not required.

It is also important to note that there is no difference between a medical transcription service and an independent contractor. If you are an independent contractor, you *are* a service owner and should be doing for your clients all of the things a service owner would do for his or hers.

Sample policies are offered below. Each can be adapted to your particular work environment.

Privacy Officer Policy

A policy for a privacy officer should clearly describe his or her duties and responsibilities. It also should state that the privacy officer is the "go-to" person for all complaints related to possible breaches of privacy. If you manage a medical transcription service company, you should have a privacy officer. If you are an independent contractor, you will be the official privacy officer for your business. If you are a medical transcriptionist who works in a hospital or physician's office, your privacy officer will be identified in your employee policies and procedures manual.

Don't let creation of policies weigh you down. You can do this!

Sample privacy officer policy

> The privacy officer is to be responsible for coordinating all activities that relate to protecting the privacy of individually identifiable health information as it pertains to the laws and regulations. The duties of the privacy officer include:
>
> 1. Creating and updating policies related to the HIPAA Privacy Rule and the protection of patient privacy for our organization.

2. Ensuring that all policies and documents reflect state laws and areas where preemption may apply.

3. Providing training about the Privacy Rule for all members of the workforce and maintaining records of the training completed.

4. Serving as the point of contact for anyone wishing to file a complaint or register a concern regarding a possible breach of privacy.

Policy for the Use of Protected Health Information

A policy should clearly outline how protected health information is to be used. It should state that every reasonable effort will be made to maintain the privacy of that information and that only the minimally necessary information will be used for all tasks. The need for such a policy is the same, whether you are an employee of a covered entity, a transcription service, or an independent contractor.

Sample policy for the use of protected health information

The health information maintained by our organization will be utilized in the manner intended: to provide patient-care documentation, to conduct on-going healthcare operations, and to conduct the daily business of the organization. The information will not be accessed for any purpose other than to ensure quality transcription of the patient's record. Access to this information will be limited to a need-to-know basis and strongly protected. At all times, the information will be protected so as to ensure the privacy of the patient whose information we use.

Policy for the Use of Protected Health Information in Quality Assurance and Educational Programs

If you have a formal quality assurance program, you will need this policy. As you may know, quality assurance editors are given access to protected health information in order to perform their jobs. How they give feedback to you should be addressed in a written policy.

The Privacy Rule also allows protected health information to be used in educational settings for the purposes of training. Note: If you are an independent contractor and you do not have a formal quality assurance program, you probably do not need this policy, unless an educational program allows you to work with student interns. Then, you would need a policy similar to the example offered below.

Protected health information must be available only on a need-to-know basis.

Sample policy for the use of protected health information in quality assurance and educational programs

Quality assurance editors will be given access to protected health information to train new employees, to conduct routine quality reviews, to perform editing of transcribed documents, and to research patient information. The editors will not access any information in addition to what is minimally necessary to perform their daily tasks.

Providing feedback to the medical transcriptionist is an important function of the quality assurance editor. All feedback will be given only after the editor has removed demographic information from the document. When quality assurance feedback must be sent to a remote location, it should be sent via secure encrypted e-mail or an alternative method that ensures the protection of the information.

Student interns may access protected health information in the course of their education and will be required to abide by all policies related to protection of the information.

Training Policy

A training policy should specify when training will be done. It should include training for all members of a workforce at the time they are put into their roles, when their roles change, and whenever policy changes impact their roles. The policy should also include a statement about the documentation required for all training.

Two sample policies follow. The first is for the workforce of covered entities and employees of medical transcription service companies. The other is for independent contractors.

Document your training sessions to show your efforts to comply.

Sample training policy

All new employees will receive Privacy Rule training that covers topics based on their role in the organization. Ongoing training will be provided at any time there is a change in policy related to their roles. Training will be documented and records maintained to show who attended the training, the topics of the training, dates, and whether the training was for a new employee or based on a policy change. If business associates are utilized, they will be required to provide documentation of the training provided to their workers.

Sample training policy for independent contractors

Training sessions will be attended to be sure that I am knowledgeable about the requirements for the Privacy Rule. This will include keeping myself informed of changes in the Privacy Rule and how it impacts my business. I will maintain documentation of this training, should any client require verification. In addition, if I use subcontractors, I will keep records to verify they have attended training sessions related to the Privacy Rule.

Computer Security Policy

Anyone who works with protected health information on a computer needs a computer security policy. *At a minimum,* the Privacy Rule requires a computer security policy to include four points: The first is that access to protected health information is controlled. Next is that unique identifiers are used and passwords are never shared, expire periodically, and must be reset. Third is that all computer systems are to be protected with the most up-to-date anti-virus software. And, finally, the policy should state that all operating systems are kept up to date.

Two sample policies follow. The first applies to the employee setting, whether the medical transcriptionist works in a hospital or for a medical transcription service. The second is for independent contractors.

Sample computer security policy

In the course of performing medical transcription for a patient's record, transcriptionists are provided access to confidential client and patient information. The safeguarding of this confidential information is the primary responsibility of everyone employed by the organization. Federal law requires us to ensure the security of confidential personally identifiable medical information including, but not limited to, the patient's name, address, and financial and diagnostic information. To ensure compliance with federal requirements, we reserve the right to audit the work and systems used by our employees in the performance of their duties. As an employee, you must:

1. Maintain and use the most current version of virus protection software.

2. Perform routine operating system updates as instructed by the information systems department.

3. Not save, in any form, information accessed on the computer or files of a client.

4. Return or shred any information printed during the course of performing your job duties.

5. Never access your own information or the information of someone you know personally. You must only access those accounts assigned to you. Accessing information for personal reasons is grounds for immediate dismissal.

Be sure you dish up a healthy respect for protecting every patient's privacy.

6. Never alter, change, update, or delete any authentic contents of computers or files unless properly authorized to do so.

7. Only perform activities associated with your job function or responsibilities.

8. Only access computers or files on a need-to-know basis.

9. Immediately notify your manager if someone asks you to improperly alter information.

10. Immediately notify your manager if you learn of or have reason to believe any employee is performing unauthorized access, disclosure, alteration, change, update, or deletion of information stored in computers or files.

11. Never disclose your password to anyone (other than your immediate manager or the systems staff when requested) for any reason. Your password and user name provide your own unique identification for computer access. You are personally responsible for your computer access.

12. Never allow others to access any computer with your user name and password.

13. Never allow anyone other than another employee who is performing his or her job duties to view your computer screen while in use.

14. Never store your password where others can see it.

15. Never leave your computer logged on and accessible while unattended. Log off your computer when unattended, even if you are leaving for only a short break.

16. Never allow company-owned equipment to be used by anyone other than yourself or other employees.

17. Never allow access to patient files by others, when your own (home) computer is being used to perform your job.

18. Immediately return work upon completion. No copy should be stored on the hard drive. When protected health information is retained until the client/service acknowledges receipt and payment is received, then it should be removed from the computer, transferred to disk/CD, and stored securely in a fireproof locked cabinet or receptacle. Once receipt is acknowledged and payment received, the media should then be appropriately destroyed. Work logs should be handled in the same manner.

19. Remove all protected health information from the computer hard drive when the computer must be repaired. If a hard drive is replaced, the medical transcriptionist should ensure that the old hard drive is destroyed. A record should be kept of those who made the repairs.

Violation of these policies will result in appropriate disciplinary action, up to and including termination, and could lead to prosecution under the Health Insurance Portability and Accountability Act (HIPAA), the Computer Fraud and Abuse Act, or other state and federal laws.

Sample computer security policy for independent contractors

In the course of performing medical transcription for a patient's record, transcriptionists are provided access to confidential client and patient information. The safeguarding of this confidential information is the primary responsibility of everyone employed by the organization. Federal law requires us to ensure the security of confidential personally identifiable medical information including, but not limited to, the patient's name, address, and financial and diagnostic information. To ensure compliance with federal requirements, I will take the following steps related to computer safety:

1. Maintain and use the most current version of virus protection software.
2. Perform routine operating system updates as instructed by the client's information systems department.
3. Not save, in any form, information accessed on the computer or files of a client.
4. Return or shred any information printed during the course of performing my job duties.
5. Never access my own information or the information of someone I know personally. I will only access those accounts assigned to me.
6. Never alter, change, update, or delete any authentic contents of computers or files unless properly authorized to do so.
7. Only perform activities associated with my job function or responsibilities.
8. Only access computers or files on a need-to-know basis.
9. Immediately notify the client if someone asks me to improperly alter information.
10. Never disclose my password to anyone for any reason.
11. Never allow anyone to view my computer screen while in use.
12. Never store passwords where others can see them.

13. Never leave the computer logged on and accessible while unattended.

14. Never allow access to patient files by others.

15. Return work immediately upon completion. Copies will only be stored on the hard drive until verification of delivery and billing. Protected health information will be retained until the client/service acknowledges receipt and payment is received and will be removed from the computer, transferred to disk/CD, and stored securely in a fireproof locked cabinet or receptacle. Once receipt is acknowledged and payment received, the media will then be appropriately destroyed. Work logs will be handled in the same manner.

16. Remove all protected health information from the computer hard drive when the computer must be repaired. If a hard drive is replaced, I will ensure that the old hard drive is destroyed. A record will be kept of those who made the repairs.

Policy for Confidentiality Agreements

All medical transcriptionists should sign a confidentiality agreement with their employer or client. If transcription is outsourced, the policy should require that all medical transcriptionists performing work for the outside service also will sign annual confidentiality agreements. A sample policy (below) and a sample confidentiality agreement (Figure 3.5) are offered here. Note that in the agreement an independent contractor would need to use a personal name where a company name would be written.

Remember to review your confidentiality agreements annually.

Sample policy for confidentiality agreements

Every medical transcriptionist, whether an employee or a contractor, including independent contractors, will sign a confidentiality agreement. It will also be signed by anyone who has access to protected health information for performing the duties of his or her job description. This agreement will be renewed on an annual basis.

Figure 3.5 Example of a Confidentiality Agreement.

Confidentiality Agreement

(Company name) _____ has a legal and ethical responsibility to safeguard the privacy of all patients and protect the confidentiality of their health information. In the course of employment with (company name) _____, I may come into contact with confidential patient information.

I understand that such information must be maintained in the strictest confidence. As a condition of my employment, I agree that, during and after my employment, I will neither disclose any patient information to any persons whatsoever nor allow any person to examine or make copies of any patient information other than as necessary in the course of my employment. When patient information must be discussed with other health-care workers in the course of my work, I will use discretion to ensure that such conversations cannot be overheard by others who are not involved in the patient's care.

I understand that violation of this agreement may result in disciplinary action, up to and including termination of employment.

Employee Signature: _____

Date: _____

Policy for Work Area Arrangements

The steps necessary to secure protected health information in a work area should be outlined in a policy. The policy should address where the computer is located, what happens when the computer is not in use, and how to handle voice files. Two sample policies follow. The first is for the company office setting. The second is for a home office setting.

Sample policy for work area arrangements in an office setting

All medical transcription work areas must be secure in such a manner as to protect the health information processed in that work area. In order to accomplish this:

//// **CAUTION** ////

Medical transcriptionists often assist each other by listening to difficult phrases in a dictation. If the phrase contains protected health information, be sure not to play it over a speaker. You could breach the patient's privacy by doing so.

1. Set screen savers on your computers, so that they are activated after two minutes of inactivity.

2. Position computer screens so they face away from all public areas.

3. Log out of the system when leaving your work station for any reason. Do not leave protected health information on the screen for others to access.

4. Never play portions of voice files that contain protected health information over a speaker. Always use headsets even when asking a coworker to assist you by listening to a portion of the file.

5. File copies containing patient information, such as census sheets or schedules, in a locked cabinet when they are not being utilized. They should never be left on a desk unattended.

Sample policy for work area arrangements in a home office setting

The following policy applies to both home-based employees of a covered entity or medical transcription service, as well as to independent contractors.

All medical transcription work areas must be secure in such a manner as to protect the health information processed in that work area. In order to accomplish this:

1. Set screen savers on your computers, so that they are activated after two minutes of inactivity.

2. Position computer screens so they are unavailable to those entering your work area, including family.

3. Log out of the system when leaving your work station for any reason. Do not leave protected health information on the screen for others to access.

4. Never play portions of voice files that contain protected health information over a speaker.

5. Place file copies containing patient information, such as census sheets or schedules, in a locked cabinet when they are not being utilized. They should never be left on a desk unattended.

Access Policy for Digital Dictation Systems

A policy on how to access a digital dictation system should be similar to a policy for computer system access. However, it also should include guidelines on the use of cell phones for dictation. If you are a medical transcription service owner or an independent contractor and have your own digital dictation system, you will want to include this policy in your policy manual. If you access a client's system to transcribe voice files, it is a good idea to ask the client for a copy of his or her policy, so that you are fully aware of your responsibilities.

Sample access policy for digital dictation systems

> Digital dictation systems are to be protected under the computer security policy. Because the use of cellular phones is not secure, it is the policy of this institution to request that they not be used to dictate confidential medical information (optional, depending on facility policies). Each user will be given a unique identifier and password for access. Passwords to access the dictation system are never to be shared, either by the medical transcriptionist or the healthcare provider using the system to dictate medical reports. Voice files transferred from the dictation system are to be transferred through secure sites in order to protect the information.

Policy for the Use of Hard Copy Protected Health Information

Medical transcriptionists often use hard copies of patient information in order to verify demographics. These hard copies must be shredded (not thrown in a wastebasket) when they are no longer needed to perform transcription.

Sample policy for the use of hard copy protected health information

Medical transcriptionists, in the course of performing their duties, may need to access hard copy protected health information, such as schedules, census sheets, and so on. This information is not to be left on any desk unattended where others could access the information. Upon completion of use, the copies are to be shredded immediately.

Policy for Use of the Fax Machine

A policy for use of a fax machine should address its location and how and when a fax containing protected health information may be sent. It should also address the proper way to handle incoming faxes and what to do when a fax is sent or received in error. Figure 3.6 shows an example of a fax cover sheet that includes the required confidentiality clause.

The following policy may be implemented in any work setting, whether it involves employees or independent contractors.

Sample policy for use of the fax machine

Protected health information may be transmitted via fax machine only when necessary to ensure patient care. Such machines must be located in a private area, not a public one. All faxes are to be transmitted with a fax cover sheet. Preprogrammed numbers will be utilized when possible. Fax numbers will be verified prior to transmission. Also, prior to transmission, the sender will verify that the person who is to receive the fax is available to receive it, so that it will not be

---

Figure 3.6 Example of a Fax Cover Sheet.

Fax Cover Sheet

To: _____

Organization:_____

Fax Number:_____

Voice Number: _____

From:_____

Organization: _____

Fax Number: _____

Voice Number: _____

Total pages, including cover sheet: _____

Subject: _____

IMPORTANT WARNING: This message is intended for the use of the person or entity to which it is addressed and may contain information that is privileged and confidential, the disclosure of which is governed by applicable law. If the reader of this message is not the intended recipient, or the employee or agent responsible to deliver it to the intended recipient, you are hereby notified that any dissemination, distribution, or copying of this information is STRICTLY PROHIBITED. If you have received this message by error, please notify us immediately and destroy the related message.

---

left unattended on the receiver's fax machine. All faxes sent are to be maintained in a log that notes date, time, recipient, fax number, and confirmation that the fax was received.

When receiving a fax containing protected health information, the fax is to be removed from the machine immediately and processed. It is not to be left unattended on the fax machine where other persons can access the information.

If a fax containing protected health information is received in error, the sender will be notified immediately. The fax will be noted on the log sheet used to track incoming faxed documents. The documents transmitted in error will be shredded immediately.

E-Mail Policy

An e-mail policy should clearly state whether or not e-mail transmission of protected health information is permissible within your

Stay the course. You're halfway there.

organization. When protected health information is allowed to be transmitted via e-mail, seriously consider using an encrypted system. The Privacy Rule does not require encryption. However, it is recommended and may be considered by the law as a reasonable effort to secure protected health information. Two sample policies are offered below. The first pertains to employees. The second is for independent contractors.

Sample policy for use of e-mail for employees

Computers, computer files, e-mail, voice mail, Internet access, and software furnished to employees are intended for business use only. Attachments to e-mail are to be scanned for viruses prior to opening. The systems department will instruct you on proper scanning procedures.

All non-business e-mails, such as jokes, cartoons, and other personal e-mail, are to be deleted. In addition, any attachments to personal e-mail must not be scanned *or opened* under any circumstances.

Before loading or downloading onto any computer, all diskettes, CDs (including new ones out of the box), and computer programs are to be scanned for viruses and software attachments by a member of the systems department.

Every reasonable effort is to be taken to protect the privacy and confidentiality of protected health information. Therefore, all e-mails containing protected health information, patient schedules, demographics, quality assurance feedback, and e-mails to clients are to be encrypted before sending.

E-mails always are to have the following statement attached: "IMPORTANT WARNING! This message is intended for the use of the person or entity to which it is addressed and may contain information that is privileged and confidential, the disclosure of which is governed by applicable law. If the reader of this message is not the intended recipient or the employee or agent responsible to deliver it to the intended recipient, you are hereby notified that any dissemination, distribution, or copying of this information is STRICTLY PROHIBITED. If you have received this message by error, please notify us immediately and destroy the related message."

Employees are to notify their immediate supervisor or any member of management upon learning of violations of this policy. Employees who violate this policy will be subject to disciplinary action, up to and including termination of employment.

Sample policy for use of e-mail for independent contractors

All attachments to e-mail will be scanned for viruses prior to opening.

Every reasonable effort is to be taken to protect the privacy and confidentiality of protected health information. Therefore, it is a business practice that all e-mails containing protected health information, patient schedules, demographics, quality assurance feedback, and e-mails to clients will be encrypted before sending.

E-mails always are to have the following statement attached: "IMPORTANT WARNING! This message is intended for the use of the person or entity to which it is addressed and may contain information that is privileged and confidential, the disclosure of which is governed by applicable law. If the reader of this message is not the intended recipient or the employee or agent responsible to deliver it to the intended recipient, you are hereby notified that any dissemination, distribution, or copying of this information is STRICTLY PROHIBITED. If you have received this message by error, please notify us immediately and destroy the related message."

Disaster Recovery Policy

This policy should outline how your organization would recover protected health information in the case of a disaster. It should state that backup systems are used to protect private health information. It should outline who is responsible for maintaining the system, how often backups are per-

Here's a Hint

Remember, with e-mail:

E *Every*

M *Message*

A *Always*

I *Includes a*

L *Legal privacy warning!*

formed, and how information will be retrieved in the case of a disaster. Two sample policies follow. The first is for covered entities and medical transcription services. The second is for individual independent contractors.

Sample disaster recovery policy for covered entities and medical transcription services

> All computer systems are to be attached to the appropriate UPS and surge protectors to guard against damage from lightning and power spikes. The transcription systems for both transcribed documents and voice recorders are to be backed up daily. The maintenance of backups is the responsibility of the information systems manager, who is to store backups in a secure environment where they are accessible should a system need to be rebuilt. Software applications that have an automatic backup setting should be set to back up data every two to five minutes. In the event of a disaster that shuts down the system, the information systems manager will be responsible for coordinating and assisting with recovery of data.

Sample disaster recovery policy for independent contractors

If you are an independent contractor and you do not have an information systems manager, you will be responsible for disaster recovery yourself. You may choose to contract this out, so that your records are backed up and stored away from your office. At a minimum, you should be backing up your data to a CD on a daily basis. This will make recovery much easier in the event of a system failure. A sample disaster recovery policy for you follows:

You never know when your backup plan will be needed so be prepared.

All computer systems will be attached to the appropriate UPS and surge protectors. Transcribed documents and voice recorders will be backed up daily. Software applications that have an automatic back up setting will be set to back up every two to five minutes.

Policy for Offsite Medical Transcriptionists

Medical transcriptionists are often located offsite, whether working for a hospital or a medical transcription service and either as an employee or as an independent contractor. Policies need to be created that describe any additional items that the offsite medical transcriptionist must do in his or her work environment to be compliant with the Privacy Rule.

Sample policy for offsite medical transcriptionists

Offsite medical transcriptionists are to be held to the same policies as those who work onsite. Additional safeguards include:

1. *Physical Media:* Information on audiocassette or other media (disks) is to be shipped or mailed only by a carrier who can track the shipment and who will not deliver unless a designated recipient signs a receipt. When not in use, the offsite medical transcriptionist is to store such media in a locked fireproof receptacle/storage cabinet.

2. *Access to Voice Files and Demographic Databases:* Passwords are to be required for access. The offsite medical transcriptionist is responsible for maintaining confidentiality by never sharing passwords or access and always logging out of databases or transcription platforms when finished. Each person is accountable for all activity under his or her password and account.

3. *Offsite Computer Security:* If transcription is done on a company- or institution-owned computer, the owner of the computer is responsible for securing it (as in the computer security policy). If transcription is done on a medical transcriptionist-owned computer, then:

   a. The medical transcriptionist must provide the employer or client with a signed statement ensuring that the computer used to process protected health information is a work tool that is not shared by family members. If this is not possible, the medical transcriptionist must provide assurance that acceptable measures have been taken to

ensure patient confidentiality, such as password protected folders and encrypted files. Passwords must be
kept secure and should be changed frequently (see Disaster Recovery section below). Also recommended are a
password-protected screen saver and the habit of locking the computer whenever one steps away from it.

b. The medical transcriptionist must have a basic working
knowledge of the hardware/software programs used.

c. Computers with Internet access should have active firewalls in place to prevent others from gaining access to
the computer without the medical transcriptionist's
knowledge.

d. Anti-virus programs, operating systems, and spyware
detection software is to be kept up to date with periodic
upgrades as recommended by the manufacturer.

e. Updates are to be performed manually when necessary.
The automatic update capability of any software in the
computer should be turned off.

f. Software programs that allow file sharing such as games
and music programs are not to be installed on any computer where protected health information is used.

g. Work is to be returned immediately upon completion,
and no copy should be stored on the hard drive. When
protected health information is retained until the
client/service acknowledges receipt and payment is received, then it should be removed from the computer,
transferred to disk/CD, and stored securely in a fireproof locked cabinet or receptacle. Once receipt is acknowledged and payment received, the media should
then be appropriately destroyed. Work logs are to be
handled in the same manner.

h. If computer equipment must be repaired, all protected
health information should be removed from the computer hard drive. If a hard drive is replaced, the medical
transcriptionist is to be certain that the old hard drive is
destroyed. A record should be kept of who made the
repairs.

4. *Disaster Recovery/Backup Planning:* Precautions should
be taken for equipment failure and adverse environmental
conditions such as power outages.

a. Set software applications that have automatic backup
features to a frequency of two to five minutes.

b. Use surge protectors for computers and other devices
such as transcribers, including both electrical connections and phone line connections.

c. Use a UPS backup power supply for computers, so that medical transcriptionists have minutes necessary to save documents in the event of a power outage.

d. On a daily basis, back up text files to a removable backup device (such as floppy disk or CD) when work needs to be re-sent in case of computer failure.

e. Routinely back up any voice files that have not been transcribed to a second computer or removable media in case of computer failure.

> **CAUTION**
>
> An increased number of medical transcriptionists now work in home offices. Ideally, no one will have access to the medical transcriptionist's computer except the medical transcriptionist herself. However unintended, family members could gain access to her computer and protected health information. Prevent that from happening. Use password protected partitions and folders to guarantee the privacy of the protected health information.

f. When a digital dictation system is used, develop an alternate method of dictation (such as hand-held recorders).

g. Develop an alternate method for returning work if the usual manner is not available, such as if Internet access is unavailable.

h. The offsite medical transcriptionist's employer or medical transcription service owner should always have updated computer passwords in case the medical transcriptionist is incapacitated. The offsite medical transcriptionist must provide an emergency contact person who can physically access the work area and computer. In an emergency, the employer or medical transcription service owner is to give the emergency contact the passwords and have all protected health information that is retained by the medical transcriptionist retrieved or destroyed. If tapes are used, the emergency contact person should be aware of where untyped tapes are kept, so that they can be returned to the employer or medical transcription service owner immediately. In the event of the medical transcriptionist's death or permanent disability, sending the computer to the employer or medical transcription service owner for removal of protected health information is recommended.

5. *Contract Termination:* Upon termination, the medical transcriptionist is to provide certification that all protected health information and demographic information has been appropriately returned and/or destroyed.

6. *Security/Privacy Breach:* In the case of unauthorized disclosure or theft of protected health information or hardware, the employer, medical transcription company, or client is to be notified immediately. Steps must be taken to

ensure that further breaches will not occur, and these steps must be documented for the covered entity.

Don't let the idea of applying policies give you a rainy day feeling. You know this stuff!

Termination Policy

When a person leaves an organization, steps must be taken to remove his or her access to protected health information. In the case of an offsite transcriptionist, the organization should require verification that all protected health information has either been deleted from his or her computer or returned to the facility. (See an example of a medical transcriptionist termination checklist, Figure 3.7.)

Two sample policies follow. The first is for employees. The second is for independent contractors.

Sample termination policy for employees

Upon termination of either employment or a contractual arrangement, a Medical Transcriptionist Termination Checklist is to be completed, ensuring that all steps have been taken. All files containing protected health information are to be returned and/or deleted from the medical transcriptionist's computer. The system administrator will disable all passwords and access to systems. All keys that allow access to the workplace must be returned to Human Resources. Human Resources is responsible for ensuring that the proper documentation is obtained and placed in the employee's or contractor's file.

Sample termination policy for independent contractors

Upon termination of a contractual arrangement, the following steps will be performed: All files containing protected health information will be returned and/or deleted from my computer. I will request verification from the client that all passwords and access to systems assigned to me have been disabled. I will provide documentation to my client that all files

Figure 3.7 Example of a "Medical Transcriptionist Termination Checklist."

Medical Transcriptionist Termination Checklist

Employee/Contractor Full Name: _____

Mailing Address: _____

Phone: _____

Last Date Worked: _____

Task	Responsible Party	Date Completed
Instruct medical transcriptionist on back-up and deletion of files		
Send e-mail or other notice to medical transcriptionist about equipment return		
Have all keys to facility returned		
Inventory returned equipment		
Send inventory to Human Resources department for personnel folder		
Have systems administrator disable passwords		
Confirm with employee that all work-related software programs have been removed from home computer (if applicable).		

containing protected health information have been returned and/or deleted from my computer system.

Breaches and Sanctions Policies

In a perfect world, there are no breaches of protected health information. Unfortunately, the world is not perfect, and occasionally, breaches do occur. A policy should outline how these breaches will be dealt with and what steps are to be taken to ensure the breach will not occur again. Covered entities have a responsibility to lessen or alleviate any potential damage when a breach occurs, and the policy should indicate how that will be done.

If you are a medical transcription service owner or an independent contractor, learn how this particular policy works for your clients. Doing so will make it possible for you to provide the necessary documentation should a breach be the result of your actions. If you have employees, the policy should define sanctions or disciplinary action for a breach of protected health information. Consider a tiered approach to sanctions. For example, a reprimand plus retraining may be an appropriate sanction for a breach that was an honest mistake. However, that sanction would not be appropriate for someone who took information with the intent to sell it.

A breaches and sanctions policy for a covered entity will be different from one drawn up for a business associate, who has a duty to notify the covered entity at the time of any breach. Samples of both policies are offered below.

Sample breaches and sanctions policies for a covered entity

> All breaches of protected health information are to be reported immediately to the privacy officer. The privacy officer is responsible for investigating the cause of the breach, determining how to ensure it will not recur, and recommending any potential sanctions to the person responsible. Should the breach be the result of action by a business associate, the privacy officer is to seek assurance from the business associate that steps have been taken to make certain the incident will not recur. In the absence of such assurances, the contract with the business associate may be terminated.
>
> Employees who inappropriately use protected health information will be subject to disciplinary action, up to and including termination. Any employee who discloses protected health information for personal gain, with malicious intent, or with the intent of using and/or selling will be terminated immediately. The privacy officer also will make a determination about any possible harm caused by the breach and make recommendations regarding how to alleviate or lessen the damages.

Sample breaches and sanctions policies for a business associate

Note that if you are an independent contractor, the duties of the privacy officer will be your responsibility to fulfill.

In the case of a breach of information, the breach will be reported immediately to the company's privacy officer. The privacy officer will be responsible for determining how to prevent such a breach from occurring in the future. A report-of-disclosure form will be filled out, indicating what information was breached, to whom it was breached, and that the client has been notified. This form will be kept on file for six years.

The covered entity will be notified of the breach and informed of the steps that have been taken to ensure it does not recur. Employees or subcontractors who are responsible for inappropriate disclosure of protected health information shall be subject to disciplinary action, up to and including termination of employment or contract.

Any person who discloses protected health information for personal gain, with malicious intent, or with the intent of using and/or selling will be terminated (or his or her contract terminated) immediately. The privacy officer also is to make a determination about any possible harm caused by the breach and make recommendations regarding how to mitigate the damages.

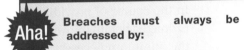

Breaches must always be addressed by:

- Notifying the client that a breach has occurred, if you are a business associate.
- Investigating the reason for the breach.
- Taking steps to ensure a similar breach will not occur in the future.
- Applying appropriate sanctions or disciplinary action to the person who committed the breach.

Complaint Policy

Complaints about problems with protected health information may come from any source. So a policy should clearly identify who is responsible for receiving such complaints. Usually, that is the privacy officer. The complaint policy should describe—for clients and for employees—the steps to take to file a complaint. A "no retaliation" statement also should be included. Though it is unlikely that a business associate would receive a complaint from a patient, it is possible that an employee may need to report a violation. A written policy should outline how the situation is to be handled.

Sample complaint policy

All complaints about the misuse or inappropriate disclosure of protected health information are to be directed to the privacy officer. The privacy officer shall investigate the complaints, determine if a breach has occurred, and make recommendations about possible sanctions as well as remedies to ensure a breach will not occur in the future. In addition, the privacy officer shall make recommendations regarding how to mitigate damages from any possible harm due to the breach. There will be no retaliation taken against any person who files a complaint, provided he or she does so in good faith and has a reasonable expectation to believe a breach has occurred.

Vendor Policy

In the course of providing a service, a vendor may have access to protected health information. This access should always be kept to the minimum necessary to complete the task. If you are a covered entity, business associate agreements should be in place for those who need to access protected health information. If you are a medical transcription service or an independent contractor, you will need a subcontractor agreement with the vendor who has access to the protected health information on your computers.

Sample vendor policy for covered entities

In the course of business, it is necessary that some vendors who provide services have access to systems containing protected health information. All vendors will sign business associate agreements and be subject to all of the restrictions contained in these agreements. Vendors will be given access only to the minimal necessary information in order to perform the duties they are contracted to perform.

Sample vendor policy for transcription service companies and independent contractors

In the course of business, it is necessary that some vendors who provide services have access to systems containing protected health information. All vendors will sign subcontractor agreements and be subject to all of the restrictions contained in these agreements. Vendors will be given access only to the minimal necessary information in order to perform the duties they are contracted to perform.

POLICIES FOR BUSINESS ASSOCIATES

A policy for business associates should state that the relationship with a client is to be clearly defined within a business associate agreement. For a covered entity, the policy should state this agreement must be in place before work may begin. It should also explain how the business associate will meet his or her obligations. Special attention also should be given to the instructions for how potential breaches are to be handled. A sample policy follows:

Aha! What is the easiest way for a covered entity to determine if a contractor or vendor is a business associate and needs a business associate agreement? They ask this question: "Does the contractor or vendor have access to protected health information in performing a service?" If the answer is "yes," the contractor or vendor is a business associate. If the answer is no, then no business associate agreement is required.

> All business associates are to sign a formal business associate agreement. They also are to be required to ensure, as a part of the agreement, that any subcontractors who they engage will be subject to the same agreement and the restrictions within that agreement. All business associate agreements are to require full disclosure regarding where the work is performed. Business associate agreements are to be reviewed on an annual basis.

Should a breach of the privacy of protected health information occur as a result of the actions of the business associate, the breach will be investigated as to its nature and to the steps that will be taken in the future to ensure it will not recur. If reasonable assurance is not given that a breach will not recur, the business associate arrangement will be terminated. Business associates will also be requested to take steps to assist a covered entity in mitigating damages from any harm that may occur as a result of a breach caused by the business associate or his or her subcontractors.

Note that while the Privacy Rule does not require it, covered entities would be wise to require their business associates to provide full disclosure about where work is performed. Many times medical transcription is sent offshore to be performed. There is no restriction in the Privacy Rule that prohibits this. However, to decide if that is a risk worth taking, an informed decision must be made.

Sample Contracts and Agreements

Aha! Contracts may be initiated by anyone—a covered entity or a business associate, a client or an independent contractor. It does not matter who writes it, as long as the required topics are included in it.

By now, each business associate, whether a transcription service or an independent contractor, should have a business associate agreement in place. If you do not, do it now, so that you and your clients can be sure you are both compliant with the rule. Failure to address this issue could mean that you will have limited business opportunities.

The Privacy Rule requires a covered entity to have a business associate agreement with each organization that provides a service requiring access to protected health information. The rule outlines very specific items to be included in the agreement. It says the agreement must state that the business associate will:

1. Not use or disclose protected health information in any manner other than what is permitted by the agreement or required by law.

2. Use appropriate safeguards to protect against unauthorized use or disclosure of protected health information.

3. Report to the covered entity any use or disclosure not allowed by the agreement.

4. Ensure that any agent or subcontractor agrees to the same restrictions as the business associate.

5. Make protected health information available as necessary for the covered entity, so that it may comply with its obligations to patients and others under HIPAA.

6. Make available to the Secretary of the Department of Health and Human Services the business associate's internal practices, records, and books relating to the use and disclosure of protected health information.

7. Destroy or return to the covered entity, if possible, all protected health information when the agreement is terminated. If it is not possible, then the protection of the information under the agreement must apply for as long as the business associate keeps the information. The business associate is not allowed to use or disclose that information except for the reasons for which

it was kept. (An example would be a contract that is terminated, but payment for work performed has not yet been received. The business associate would be allowed to keep the documents containing protected health information until payment is received. Then, the protected health information must be returned or destroyed.)

There are two ways to handle the requirements for a business associate agreement: (1) they may be offered as a separate document or (2) the language specific to the Privacy Rule may be included in the regular contract for services. This is simply a matter of preference and either is acceptable. Examples of both options are offered below.

Sample business associate agreement

The Office of Civil Rights, Department of Health and Human Services, has prepared a sample business associate contract. That sample is provided below. As with any contractual agreement, it should be reviewed by legal counsel before use.

MEDICAL PRIVACY—NATIONAL STANDARDS TO PROTECT THE PRIVACY OF PERSONAL HEALTH INFORMATION

Sample Business Associate Contract Provisions

[Published in FR 67 No. 157 pg. 53182, 53264 (August 14, 2002)]

STATEMENT OF INTENT

The Department provides these sample business associate contract provisions in response to numerous requests for guidance. This is only sample language. These provisions are designed to help covered entities more easily comply with the business associate contract requirements of the Privacy Rule. However, use of these sample provisions is not required for compliance with the Privacy Rule. The language may be amended to more accurately reflect business arrangements between the covered entity and the business associate.

These or similar provisions may be incorporated into an agreement for the provision of services between the entities or they may be incorporated into a separate business associate agreement. These provisions only address concepts and requirements set forth in the Privacy Rule and alone are not sufficient to result in a binding contract under State law. They do not include many formalities and substantive provisions that are required or typically included in a valid contract. Reliance on this sample is not sufficient for compliance with State law and does not replace consultation with a lawyer or negotiations between the parties to the contract.

Furthermore, a covered entity may want to include other provisions that are related to the Privacy Rule but that are not required by the Privacy Rule. For example, a covered entity may want to add provisions in a business associate contract in order for the covered entity to be able to rely on the business associate to help the covered entity meet its obligations under the Privacy Rule. In addition, there may be permissible uses or disclosures by a business associate that are not specifically addressed in these sample provisions, for example having a business associate create a limited data set. These and other types of issues will need to be worked out between the parties.

SAMPLE BUSINESS ASSOCIATE CONTRACT PROVISIONS[1]

Definitions (alternative approaches)

Catch-all definition:

Terms used, but not otherwise defined, in this Agreement shall have the same meaning as those terms in the Privacy Rule.

Examples of specific definitions:

a. Business Associate. "Business Associate" shall mean

b. Covered Entity. "Covered Entity" shall mean

c. Individual. "Individual" shall have the same meaning as the term "individual" in 45 CFR § 164.501 and shall include a person who qualifies as a personal representative in accordance with 45 CFR § 164.502(g).

d. Privacy Rule. "Privacy Rule" shall mean the Standards for Privacy of Individually Identifiable Health Information at 45 CFR Part 160 and Part 164, Subparts A and E.

e. Protected Health Information. "Protected Health Information" shall have the same meaning as the term "protected health information" in 45 CFR § 164.501, limited to the information created or received by Business Associate from or on behalf of Covered Entity.

f. Required By Law. "Required By Law" shall have the same meaning as the term "required by law" in 45 CFR § 164.501.

g. Secretary. "Secretary" shall mean the Secretary of the Department of Health and Human Services or his designee.

Obligations and Activities of Business Associate

a. Business Associate agrees to not use or disclose Protected Health Information other than as permitted or required by the Agreement or as Required By Law.

---

[1] Words or phrases contained in brackets are intended as either optional language or as instructions to the users of these sample provisions and are not intended to be included in the contractual provisions.

b. Business Associate agrees to use appropriate safeguards to prevent use or disclosure of the Protected Health Information other than as provided for by this Agreement

c. Business Associate agrees to mitigate, to the extent practicable, any harmful effect that is known to Business Associate of a use or disclosure of Protected Health Information by Business Associate in violation of the requirements of this Agreement. [This provision may be included if it is appropriate for the Covered Entity to pass on its duty to mitigate damages to a Business Associate.]

d. Business Associate agrees to report to Covered Entity any use or disclosure of the Protected Health Information not provided for by this Agreement of which it becomes aware.

e. Business Associate agrees to ensure that any agent, including a subcontractor, to whom it provides Protected Health Information received from, or created or received by Business Associate on behalf of Covered Entity agrees to the same restrictions and conditions that apply through this Agreement to Business Associate with respect to such information.

f. Business Associate agrees to provide access, at the request of Covered Entity, and in the time and manner [Insert negotiated terms], to Protected Health Information in a Designated Record Set, to Covered Entity or, as directed by Covered Entity, to an Individual in order to meet the requirements under 45 CFR § 164.524. [Not necessary if business associate does not have protected health information in a designated record set.]

g. Business Associate agrees to make any amendment(s) to Protected Health Information in a Designated Record Set that the Covered Entity directs or agrees to pursuant to 45 CFR § 164.526 at the request of Covered Entity or an Individual, and in the time and manner [Insert negotiated terms]. [Not necessary if business associate does not have protected health information in a designated record set.]

h. Business Associate agrees to make internal practices, books, and records, including policies and procedures and Protected Health Information, relating to the use and disclosure of Protected Health Information received from, or created or received by Business Associate on behalf of, Covered Entity available [to the Covered Entity, or] to the Secretary, in a time and manner [Insert negotiated terms] or designated by the Secretary, for purposes of the Secretary determining Covered Entity's compliance with the Privacy Rule.

i. Business Associate agrees to document such disclosures of Protected Health Information and information related to such disclosures as would be required for Covered Entity to respond to a request by an Individual for an accounting of disclosures of Protected Health Information in accordance with 45 CFR § 164.528.

j. Business Associate agrees to provide to Covered Entity or an In-dividual, in time and manner [Insert negotiated terms], information collected in accordance with Section [Insert Section Number in Contract Where Provision (i) Appears] of this Agreement, to permit Covered Entity to respond to a request by an Individual for an accounting of disclosures of Protected Health Information in accordance with 45 CFR § 164.528.

<u>Permitted Uses and Disclosures by Business Associate</u>
<u>General Use and Disclosure Provisions [(a) and (b) are alternative approaches]</u>

a. <u>Specify purposes</u>:

Except as otherwise limited in this Agreement, Business Associate may use or disclose Protected Health Information on behalf of, or to provide services to, Covered Entity for the following purposes, if such use or disclosure of Protected Health Information would not violate the Privacy Rule if done by Covered Entity or the minimum necessary policies and procedures of the Covered Entity:
[List Purposes]

b. <u>Refer to underlying services agreement</u>:

Except as otherwise limited in this Agreement, Business Associate may use or disclose Protected Health Information to perform functions, activities, or services for, or on behalf of, Covered Entity as specified in [Insert Name of Services Agreement], provided that such use or disclosure would not violate the Privacy Rule if done by Covered Entity or the minimum necessary policies and procedures of the Covered Entity.

<u>Specific Use and Disclosure Provisions [only necessary if parties wish to allow Business Associate to engage in such activities]</u>

a. Except as otherwise limited in this Agreement, Business Associate may use Protected Health Information for the proper management and administration of the Business Associate or to carry out the legal responsibilities of the Business Associate.

b. Except as otherwise limited in this Agreement, Business Associate may disclose Protected Health Information for the proper management and administration of the Business Associate, provided that disclosures are Required By Law, or Business Associate obtains reasonable assurances from the person to whom the information is disclosed that it will remain confidential and used or further disclosed only as Required By Law or for the purpose for which it was disclosed to the person, and the person notifies the Business Associate of any instances of which it is aware in which the confidentiality of the information has been breached.

c. Except as otherwise limited in this Agreement, Business Associate may use Protected Health Information to provide Data Aggregation services to Covered Entity as permitted by 45 CFR § 164.504(e)(2)(i)(B).

d. Business Associate may use Protected Health Information to report violations of law to appropriate Federal and State authorities, consistent with § 164.502(j)(1).

Obligations of Covered Entity
Provisions for Covered Entity to Inform Business Associate of Privacy
Practices and Restrictions [provisions dependent on business arrangement]

a. Covered Entity shall notify Business Associate of any limitation(s) in its notice of privacy practices of Covered Entity in accordance with 45 CFR § 164.520, to the extent that such limitation may affect Business Associate's use or disclosure of Protected Health Information.

b. Covered Entity shall notify Business Associate of any changes in, or revocation of, permission by Individual to use or disclose Protected Health Information, to the extent that such changes may affect Business Associate's use or disclosure of Protected Health Information.

c. Covered Entity shall notify Business Associate of any restriction to the use or disclosure of Protected Health Information that Covered Entity has agreed to in accordance with 45 CFR § 164.522, to the extent that such restriction may affect Business Associate's use or disclosure of Protected Health Information.

Permissible Requests by Covered Entity
Covered Entity shall not request Business Associate to use or disclose Protected Health Information in any manner that would not be permissible under the Privacy Rule if done by Covered Entity. [Include an exception if the Business Associate will use or disclose protected health information for, and the contract includes provisions for, data aggregation or management and administrative activities of Business Associate].

Term and Termination

a. Term. The Term of this Agreement shall be effective as of [Insert Effective Date], and shall terminate when all of the Protected Health Information provided by Covered Entity to Business Associate, or created or received by Business Associate on behalf of Covered Entity, is destroyed or returned to Covered Entity, or, if it is infeasible to return or destroy Protected Health Information, protections are extended to such information, in accordance with the termination provisions in this Section. [Term may differ.]

b. Termination for Cause. Upon Covered Entity's knowledge of a material breach by Business Associate, Covered Entity shall either:

   1. Provide an opportunity for Business Associate to cure the breach or end the violation and terminate this Agreement [and the _____ Agreement/ sections _____ of the _____ Agreement] if Business Associate does not cure the breach or end the violation within the time specified by Covered Entity;

   2. Immediately terminate this Agreement [and the _____ Agreement/ sections _____ of the _____ Agreement] if Business Associate has breached a material term of this Agreement and cure is not possible; or

   3. If neither termination nor cure are feasible, Covered Entity shall report the violation to the Secretary.

[Bracketed language in this provision may be necessary if there is an underlying services agreement. Also, opportunity to cure is permitted, but not required by the Privacy Rule.]

c.   Effect of Termination.

1.   Except as provided in paragraph (2) of this section, upon termination of this Agreement, for any reason, Business Associate shall return or destroy all Protected Health Information received from Covered Entity, or created or received by Business Associate on behalf of Covered Entity. This provision shall apply to Protected Health Information that is in the possession of subcontractors or agents of Business Associate. Business Associate shall retain no copies of the Protected Health Information.

2.   In the event that Business Associate determines that returning or destroying the Protected Health Information is infeasible, Business Associate shall provide to Covered Entity notification of the conditions that make return or destruction infeasible. Upon [Insert negotiated terms] that return or destruction of Protected Health Information is infeasible, Business Associate shall extend the protections of this Agreement to such Protected Health Information and limit further uses and disclosures of such Protected Health Information to those purposes that make the return or destruction infeasible, for so long as Business Associate maintains such Protected Health Information.

Miscellaneous

a.   Regulatory References. A reference in this Agreement to a section in the Privacy Rule means the section as in effect or as amended.

b.   Amendment. The Parties agree to take such action as is necessary to amend this Agreement from time to time as is necessary for Covered Entity to comply with the requirements of the Privacy Rule and the Health Insurance Portability and Accountability Act of 1996, Pub. L. No. 104-191.

c.   Survival. The respective rights and obligations of Business Associate under Section [Insert Section Number Related to "Effect of Termination"] of this Agreement shall survive the termination of this Agreement.

d.   Interpretation. Any ambiguity in this Agreement shall be resolved to permit Covered Entity to comply with the Privacy Rule.

Sample of privacy rule language added to a transcription services contract

The document below is offered as an example of how to add Privacy Rule requirements to a transcription services contract. In this sample, the services provided are defined at the beginning of the general agreement and not repeated. If services are not clearly defined early, a section identifying how protected health information is to be used would be required.

Note: If you are an independent contractor and your business does not have a name, you would substitute your personal name for the word "COMPANY" in the sample below.

HEALTH INSURANCE PORTABILITY AND ACCOUNTABILITY ACT (HIPAA) REQUIREMENTS [This section is required by federal law.]

In addition to all other representations, terms, and conditions provided in this Agreement, with respect only to the information provided by the Client or "Health Information," as defined in the Health Insurance Portability and Accountability Act, obtained by COMPANY in connection with services rendered for the Client under this Agreement, COMPANY represents and agrees as follows:

1. Definitions

    Protected Health Information means individually identifiable information (including demographic information) relating to a person's health, to the health care provided to a person, or to payment for health care.

    Terms used, but not otherwise defined, in this Agreement shall have the same meaning as those terms in 45 CFR 160.103 and 164.501.

2. Obligations and Activities of COMPANY

    COMPANY will:

    (a) not use or further disclose Protected Health Information other than as permitted or required by this Agreement or as required or permitted by law.

    (b) use appropriate safeguards to prevent use or disclosure of the Protected Health Information other than as provided for by this Agreement or as required or permitted by law.

    (c) report to Client any use or disclosure of the Protected Health Information not provided for by this Agreement.

    (d) ensure that any agent, including a subcontractor, to whom it provides Protected Health Information received from, or created or received by COMPANY on behalf of Client agrees to the same restrictions and conditions that apply through this Agreement with respect to such information.

    (e) make internal practices, books, and records relating to the use and disclosure of Protected Health Information received from, or created or received by COMPANY on behalf of Client available to the Client, or at the request of the Client to the HHS Secretary, in a time and manner designated by the Client or the HHS Secretary, for purposes of the HHS Secretary determining Client's compliance with the Privacy Rule.

(f) document such disclosures of Protected Health Information and information related to such disclosures as would be required for Client to respond to a request by an Individual for an accounting of disclosures of that Individual's Protected Health Information. It is the policy of COMPANY to not make any disclosures other than those required to carry out the purpose of this agreement. All requests for disclosures for other purposes will be directed back to the client.

(g) provide to Client, in time and manner designated by Client, information collected in accordance with Section II 2 (f) of this Agreement, to permit Client to respond to a request by an Individual for an accounting of disclosures of that Individual's Protected Health Information.

3. General Use and Disclosure Provisions except as otherwise limited in this agreement, COMPANY may:

(a) use or disclose Protected Health Information to perform functions, activities, or services for, or on behalf of, Client as specified in this Agreement, provided that such use or disclosure would not violate the Privacy Rule if done by Client.

(b) use Protected Health Information for the proper management and administration of COMPANY or to carry out the legal responsibilities of COMPANY.

(c) disclose Protected Health Information for the proper management and administration of COMPANY, provided that disclosures are permitted or required by law, or COMPANY obtains reasonable assurances from the person to whom the information is disclosed that it will remain confidential and used or further disclosed only as permitted or required by law or for the purpose for which it was disclosed to the person, and the person notifies COMPANY of any instances of which it is aware in which the confidentiality of the information has been breached.

(d) use Protected Health Information to provide Data Aggregation services to Client.

4. Permissible Requests by Client

Client shall not request COMPANY to use or disclose Protected Health Information in any manner that would not be permissible under the Privacy Rule if done by Client except that COMPANY may use or disclose protected health information for data aggregation services provided to Client; for administrative activities of COMPANY; or for any other purpose permitted or required by law.

5. Term and Termination

(a) Term. The Term of Section II of this Agreement shall be effective as of the date first signed, and shall terminate when all of the Protected Health Information provided by Client to COMPANY, or created or received by COMPANY on behalf of Client, is destroyed or returned to Client, or, if it is infeasible to return or destroy Protected Health Information, protections are extended to such information, in accordance with the termination provisions in this Section.

(b) Termination for Cause. Upon Client's knowledge of a material breach by COMPANY, Client shall: (1) provide an opportunity for COMPANY to cure the breach or end the violation and terminate this Agreement if COMPANY does not cure the breach or end the violation within the time specified by Client; or (2) immediately terminate this Agreement if COMPANY has breached a material term of this Agreement and cure is not possible.

(c) Effect of Termination.

(1) Except as required by state or federal law, upon termination of this Agreement for any reason, COMPANY shall return or destroy all Protected Health Information received from Client, or created or received by COMPANY on behalf of Client. This provision shall apply to Protected Health Information that is in the possession of subcontractors or agents of COMPANY. COMPANY shall retain no copies of the Protected Health Information.

(2) In the event that COMPANY determines that returning or destroying the Protected Health Information is infeasible, COMPANY shall provide to Client notification of the conditions that make return or destruction infeasible. Upon mutual agreement of COMPANY and Client that return or destruction of Protected Health Information is infeasible, COMPANY shall extend the protections of this Agreement to such Protected Health Information and limit further uses and disclosures of such Protected Health Information to those purposes that make the return or destruction infeasible, for so long as COMPANY maintains such Protected Health Information.

6. Miscellaneous

(a) Regulatory References. A reference in this Agreement to a section in the Privacy Rule means the section as in effect or as amended, and for which compliance is required.

(b) Amendment. COMPANY and Client agree to take such action as is necessary to amend this Agreement from time to time as is necessary for Client to comply with the requirements of the Privacy Rule and the Health Insurance Portability and Accountability Act, Public Law 104–191.

(c) Interpretation. Any ambiguity in this Agreement shall be resolved in favor of a meaning that permits Client to comply with the Privacy Rule.

Policy for Subcontractors

According to the Privacy Rule, a business associate must give assurances that his or her subcontractors or agents will uphold all of the restrictions related to use and disclosure of protected health information. In order to accomplish this goal, a separate subcontractor agreement must be drawn up. It should state that the subcontractor will not use or disclose protected health information in any manner that is not allowed by the separate business associate agreement.

If you are an independent contractor who provides services for a medical transcription service, you will need to have a subcontractor agreement that covers this information. Also, if you are an independent contractor who uses other independent contractors to help with the work you do, you will want to have subcontractor agreements with them.

The Real World

Imagine opening your e-mail to find that a transcriptionist in Pakistan wants you to pay for work you asked her to do. She goes on to say, " . . . otherwise, I will expose all of the voice files and patient records of your facility on the Internet." Attached to this e-mail threat are actual patient files.

Indeed the *San Francisco Chronicle* reported that such an e-mail was sent to the University of California, San Francisco, in October 2003. It was learned that the university's local transcription service sent work to another service in Florida, who then sent the work to Texas, who then sent it to Pakistan. Allegedly, when the service in Texas did not provide payment to the medical transcriptionist in Pakistan, the notorious e-mail was sent to the university.

Newspapers across the nation picked up the story and ran it. Websites were full of discussions about it. Legislators asked questions about how a healthcare record is created, how much offshore labor was being used, and what was being done to protect the information. Some states proposed legislation prohibiting the use of offshore labor to process any kind of health information. Some are considering the importance of requiring full disclosure of where such work is actually performed.

All of the subcontractors involved in that story should have had subcontractor agreements. But ultimately, it is the University of California, San Francisco, which is responsible for the breach, regardless of where it occurred.

Sample policy for subcontractors

All subcontractors will have a subcontractor agreement. The agreement will not allow for use or disclosure of protected health information in a manner that is not allowed by the separate business associate agreement. The agreement will ensure that the subcontractor take all steps necessary to protect the information they access in providing their services.

Offshore Transcription Policy

The Privacy Rule does not address the use of offshore contractors. Each organization should decide how it wishes to handle the use of offshore labor and address that decision within its own policies. Every organization should require full disclosure when an offshore medical transcription service is being used. Only then can the organization make an informed decision.

A Word About Disclosures

While the Privacy Rule allows for a business associate to disclose information, medical transcription services would be wise to limit their disclosures only to what is necessary to conduct business. It is not recommended that medical transcription services perform any disclosures other than to their clients. A transcribed document is not a com-

> **///// CAUTION /////**
>
> Any time a contractor or subcontractor is used, ask where the transcription is being done. Find out where the medical transcriptionists are actually doing the work. Contracts should clearly state whether or not the use of offshore contractors is allowed.

pleted document until it is authenticated by the healthcare provider who dictated it. Therefore, disclosures should only be made by the healthcare provider. Failure to adhere to this practice could lead to patients arriving at your place of business to request changes or copies of their records. In the end, the portion of the record that is held by a medical transcription service or independent contractor is not complete and should only be released by the covered entity. This provides a protection for both the service and the covered entity.

What About Indemnification?

An indemnity clause states who will be accountable for any penalties for a breach of protected health information. Hospitals and healthcare providers often request the addition of an indemnification clause in their contracts with medical transcription service providers.

The Privacy Rule does not specifically apply to business associates, so covered entities often seek to recover any fines they may incur due to a business associate's breach of information. This is usually done with an indemnification clause that states the business associate will be accountable for any fines or penalties levied against the covered entity as a result of the business associate's unauthorized use or disclosure of protected health information.

Many times a medical transcription service will approach this issue by requesting a mutual indemnification clause that covers both parties should a breach occur by the other. It is not possible to create a policy about how you will handle this since it will be dictated in contract negotiations at the time a covered entity and business associate begin their relationship.

Medical transcriptionists should consider whether or not it is necessary to carry a general liability insurance policy in their work environment. Some companies will offer a general errors-and-omissions insurance policy, which will cover a transcriptionist. In some instances, an employer's liability insurance will also cover the employee (medical transcriptionist) if the breach is not an intentional violation of policy.

Practicing without insurance is risky. The company that covers your employer may or may not cover you.

THE BOTTOM LINE

Compliance is not an overnight process. There are many areas to cover. But medical transcriptionists ultimately serve one person—the patient—and every step that ensures the protection of his or her private health information should be taken. In doing so, not only do you comply with laws and regulations, but you also provide the patient with the protection he or she expects and deserves.

Where to Start

- Perform a gap analysis to see what work needs to be done.
- Develop for your organization or individual business appropriate policies related to the Privacy Rule.
- Provide training to your employees on policies related to the Privacy Rule. If you are an independent contractor, be sure you have attended training sessions and documented them, so that you can show your clients you have this training.

Policies, Contracts, and Agreements

- Take the sample policies provided in this chapter, and adapt them where appropriate to your individual setting.
- Review your own contracts and agreements to make sure they contain appropriate Privacy Rule language.

Whether you are a business associate or not, having policies in place will provide a value-added service to your clients and go far in showing them that you are knowledgeable about the Privacy Rule and that you are supporting their efforts at compliance.

Apply It

Multiple-choice questions are offered here to help you test your understanding. Answers are provided on page 102.

1. The purpose of a gap analysis is NOT to:
   a. identify current policies and procedures.
   b. identify current business associate contracts.
   c. develop a list of policies that need to be established.
   d. cause depression regarding how much work must be done.

2. In documenting the training you provide for your workforce, records of training should NOT include which one of the following?
   a. purpose/topic of training
   b. who was trained
   c. whether training is new or due to a policy change
   d. an evaluation of the training session

3. You are a medical transcriptionist working for a medical transcription service company. If you suspect a breach of protected health information, you should report it immediately to:
   a. the health information management director.
   b. risk management.
   c. your immediate supervisor.
   d. the company's privacy officer.

4. Which one of the following is NOT required in a business associate contract?
   a. uses of protected health information
   b. clause prohibiting offshore transcription
   c. assurance that the business associate will safeguard the information
   d. assurance that all subcontractors will agree to the same restrictions as the business associate

5. Establishing policies provides:
   a. documentation on how to handle breaches.
   b. clear expectations.
   c. a method to find easier solutions to problems.
   d. all of the above.

6. Which one of the following people would most likely have access to all computer systems in a transcription department?
   a. transcription manager
   b. health information management director
   c. information systems manager
   d. all of the above

7. To be sure you have good computer security, your policy should contain:
   a. role-based rights.
   b. use of anti-virus software.
   c. routine operating system updates.
   d. all of the above.

8. In setting up your digital dictation system, your policies about access should include:
   a. unique identifiers for each user.
   b. no sharing of passwords.
   c. no use of cell phones.
   d. answers a and b above.

9. When sending a fax, you should:
   a. use a fax cover sheet with a confidentiality statement.
   b. verify the fax number before transmission.
   c. never leave documents containing protected health information unattended on a fax machine.
   d. all of the above.

10. A new transcriptionist has been hired in your department at the hospital. Who maintains the ultimate responsibility for making sure that she is trained in policies related to the Privacy Rule?
    a. the privacy officer
    b. the transcription supervisor
    c. the health information management director
    d. other medical transcriptionists in the department

11. The quality assurance team of a medical transcription service routinely provides feedback to medical transcriptionists on questions they have or blanks they have left in a report. Because the medical transcriptionists are all remote, this feedback is done via e-mail. Which one of the statements below would be considered a "reasonable effort" for the quality assurance team to take to ensure compliance with the Privacy Rule?

    a. Feedback should not contain information that identifies the patient.

    b. All e-mails containing protected health information should be encrypted.

    c. Sending patient information via e-mail is prohibited by the Privacy Rule and should not be done.

    d. Answers a and b above are reasonable efforts.

12. Your hospital has an electronic health record. You receive a call to the transcription department from a person identifying himself as a physician's secretary. He asks that you change a diagnosis in a patient's report, which has been signed by the physician, because it is incorrect. You should:

    a. make the changes because the secretary is acting on behalf of the physician.

    b. explain to the secretary that you are not authorized to make alterations to the permanent record.

    c. require that the physician dictate an addendum to his original report.

    d. notify your supervisor of the request so that the proper steps can be taken.

13. You receive a call from a physician requesting a stat report for a surgery patient. You find that the report is "hung" in a coworker's queue. This coworker has gone home for the day. Knowing that turnaround time is of utmost importance to patient care, you should:

    a. call the coworker and ask for her password, so that patient care can proceed.

    b. tell the physician that no one will be able to access the report until the next day.

c. contact the information systems department for assistance in freeing up the report.

d. access the list of passwords that is kept on a sheet in your department for situations like this.

14. You receive a call requesting that a report be faxed to another healthcare facility. The patient is now in their emergency room for treatment, and they need to have the history of the patient's recent visit to your hospital. You locate the report. Before faxing it, you should:

a. ask for the patient's permission to release the information to the other facility.

b. double check the fax numbers and name of the person who is to receive the information.

c. log the information into the fax log to provide a record of what was sent.

d. both answers b and c.

15. As a home-based medical transcriptionist, you receive copies of patient schedules from your employer, so that you have correct spellings of patient names. These copies should be handled in what manner?

a. They should be saved for 60 days as a reference to be used to verify patient names in the future.

b. They should be kept in a locked drawer when not in use and shredded when you are done with dictation from that day's visits.

c. They may be kept indefinitely as long as they are electronic and the computer is secure from access by others.

d. They may be kept on your desk in the file folder for that date in order for you to have easy access.

16. Which one of the following actions is NOT required by the Privacy Rule when a medical transcriptionist is terminated?

a. disabling all passwords and access to systems

b. making a notation in the employee's file regarding eligibility for rehire

c. checking to be sure that all keys which allow access to the facility have been returned

d. ensuring that all files containing protected health information have been returned and/or deleted from the computer

17. You are the manager of a medical transcription service. You receive a call from Client A stating that Client B's reports have been delivered to them. They are wondering what they should do with them. You MUST take which TWO of the following steps?
a. Request that Client B destroy the reports.
b. Notify Client B of the breach and the steps you are taking to ensure such a breach will not occur in the future.
c. Determine which employee sent the files to the wrong client and terminate his or her employment.
d. All of the above.

18. You recently had tests done at the hospital where you work. Your physician has not returned calls to give you the results. You have access to the hospital's system, so you can easily look up the results and take them to the physician yourself. The BEST thing for you to do is to:
a. access the reports and call the physician with the results. After all, it is your information, and you have a right to have it.
b. request that the physician contact you with your results.
c. go through the normal steps for patients who request copies of their test results.
d. change physicians because this one does not seem interested in timely information.

19. As a transcription supervisor, you have been instructed to search for an outsource service that charges a lower price than what you are currently paying. You receive one bid that is 50% lower than the others. You suspect the company is using offshore labor but feel that perhaps a "don't ask, don't tell" approach is best. You are seeking to cut your expenditures and believe if you cannot do that, your job may be in jeopardy. Because your facility has a policy against using offshore labor, you should:

a. require that each company that has submitted a bid disclose where the transcription will be performed.
b. recommend the lowest bid, so that your expenses are reduced, and your own position will not be in jeopardy.
c. contact all companies that have submitted bids to ask them to match the lowest bid.
d. continue to seek additional bids.

TA DA! You've done it.

Answers to Apply It

1. **d.** Answers "a" through "c" are among the purposes of a gap analysis.

2. **d.** An evaluation form is not necessary or suggested.

3. **d.** While it may be policy to notify each person listed, the privacy officer should always be the "go-to" person when a breach is suspected.

4. **b.** The Privacy Rule does not prohibit offshore transcription.

5. **d.** Policies define expectations as well as document how to deal with questions when they arise.

6. **c.** The information systems manager generally has access to all computer systems. The others listed would only have access to computer systems required by their roles.

7. **d.** All of these should be included in a computer security policy.

8. **d.** While cell phones may not be a secure way to transmit protected health information, they are not prohibited in the Privacy Rule.

9. **d.** All of these answers are reasonable steps to ensure protection of protected health information.

10. **a.** Training may be conducted by others in the organization, yet the privacy officer maintains the responsibility for being sure it occurs.

11. **d.** When possible, all identifying information should be removed. When sending any information containing protected health information via e-mail, encryption would be considered a reasonable effort to protect the patient's privacy.

12. d.   Any requests to alter information improperly should be reported to your immediate supervisor.

13. c.   Passwords should never be shared with anyone other than your immediate supervisor, when requested, and the information systems department. Delaying a report until the next day when patient care is relying on the availability of the information is not an option. The information systems department would be the appropriate avenue for accessing the information and freeing up the report so it can be processed.

14. d.   An authorization is not required for treatment. Therefore, no release of information would be required in order to fax this report to another healthcare facility.

15. b.   Both hard copies and electronic copies of protected health information should be destroyed when they are no longer needed to perform the transcription. Hard copies should never be kept in an open file on someone's desk.

16. b.   Answers a, c, and d are all part of the termination process policy as required by the Privacy Rule.

17.   a and b. However, depending on the nature of the breach and the reason it occurred, "c" may be appropriate. Should it be determined that this was simply an accident, termination of the responsible employee probably is too severe, but disciplinary action should be taken to document that you have dealt with the breach.

18. c.   Healthcare workers often have access to their own protected health information. Should you wish copies of your information, it can be obtained in the same manner as any patient would obtain their records.

19. a.   Though not required by the Privacy Rule, knowledge of whether or not offshore labor is being used allows a covered entity to make an informed decision on how protected health information is handled for the facility.

Frequently Asked Questions

1. *Is it legal to fax patient schedules to an offsite medical transcriptionist?*

    The Privacy Rule does not prohibit the use of a fax machine to transmit patient information. However, follow your own established policies—or the policies agreed upon by your contract with your client—to make sure that the information you fax is protected. Those policies should include having a confidentiality or privacy statement on the fax cover sheet, double checking all telephone numbers before sending the fax, and making sure that the person who is to receive the fax is aware that it is coming and is available to receive it.

2. *Does the Privacy Rule prohibit physicians from using cellular phones to dictate reports?*

    There is nothing in the Privacy Rule specific to cell phone usage. Organizations may establish their own policies on the use of cell phones to transmit patient information. However, most cell phone transmissions are not considered secure and nothing at the moment can make them so. You may want to consider a policy that does not allow cell phones to be used for dictation of patient reports.

3. *Our hospital has always taken student interns in transcription. Does the Privacy Rule now prohibit this?*

    The Privacy Rule allows access to protected health information for educational purposes. Students should sign confidentiality agreements and receive the same Privacy Rule training that employees receive.

4. *As an independent contractor, my clients expect me to maintain copies of reports forever. What does the Privacy Rule require?*

    Your contracts with clients should specify how long you will store transcribed reports. The recommendations from both the

American Association for Medical Transcription and the American Society for Testing and Materials (ASTM), (*E1902: Standard Specification for Management of the Confidentiality and Security of Dictation, Transcription, and Transcribed Health Records*), are that files are kept only as long as necessary. That usually means long enough to verify delivery of the reports to the client, to perform billing on those reports, and to receive payment. Independent contractors and medical transcription services should avoid becoming a storage facility for patient reports unless this service is clearly required in your contracts.

5. *My client wants to be listed as an "also insured" on my liability insurance policy. Does the Privacy Rule require this?*

   No. Liability insurance and/or indemnification is not required by the Privacy Rule. However, many medical transcription services are asked to provide proof of liability insurance coverage. Because civil fines can be imposed on covered entities, they want a way to recover the money when there is a breach. You may find that having this insurance is a determining factor on whether or not you get a contract with a client.

6. *We work in a physician's office. All of our dictation is on tapes, which are picked up by a medical transcriptionist. She transcribes them and then delivers the printed documents to our office. How does the Privacy Rule apply to us?*

   The Privacy Rule covers all forms of protected health information—electronic, written, and oral. You will be required to comply with all of the steps necessary to ensure that you have protected the private health information of your patients. So whether the information is on tape or on transcribed hard copy, it is to be carried in a locked box to be sure that it is protected when it travels from your office to the transcriptionist's office and back again.

7. *I am a medical transcription service owner who sends dictation over the Internet to medical transcriptionists, who transcribe the reports. I then hand deliver the work back to the client. Are audit trails required in this situation?*

   An audit trail is required for any disclosure. However, because transcription of medical documents falls into the category of "healthcare operations," the Privacy Rule does not require an audit trail. If you are a transcription service owner or an independent contractor, this kind of transmission of information is not considered a disclosure, and no audit trail is required.

8. *I manage a medical transcription service company. We use a billing service, which takes our transcribed documents, verifies counts on them, and submits bills to our clients. Is an audit trail required for the billing service to access the reports?*

    Billing for work performed falls into the category of administering business functions. No audit trail is required in this instance.

9. *Is there a minimum standard for firewall protection when connected to the Internet?*

    The Privacy Rule does not have a minimum standard for firewall protection. However, it does require that steps must be taken to protect the privacy of the information on computer systems. Firewalls make sense as a reasonable effort to accomplish this.

10. *What about shredders? I understand that a cross-cut shredder is required. Is that true?*

    The Privacy Rule does not require you to use a cross-cut shredder. Any shredder will do the trick. Just be sure to store protected health information in a secure area until it is no longer needed. Then, use any shredder that will make it impossible for someone to breach the privacy of the information after it is discarded.

11. *I often deliver tapes to and pick up transcribed reports from my subcontractors when they are not at home. Is the use of a locked mailbox or locked box on their front porch considered a secure setting?*

    Yes, but only if the locked box is securely bolted down, so that it cannot be carried away. Keys should only be given to the person who is delivering the work and to the medical transcriptionist who will retrieve it. A written record should be kept of who has keys. You will also want to be sure you get the keys returned if your delivery person changes.

12. *How can I stay informed about changes in the Privacy Rule?*

    Proposed updates to all rules are published in the *Federal Register*. Watch for and review the notice of proposed rulemaking when it is available. These updates can be found at: http://aspe.hhs.gov/admnsimp/index.shtml.

13. *I am an independent contractor with my own clients, including physicians and hospitals. It seems to me that the Privacy Rule really only applies to covered entities and medical transcription service companies. Is that true?*

    You should recognize that being an independent contractor does indeed make you a business owner. In order to maintain your clients, who consider you a business associate, you would need to do all of the things related to a business associate in the Privacy Rule.

14. *I am an independent contractor who has a contract with a medical transcription service. Does the Privacy Rule apply to me?*

    In this case, you would not need to have a business associate agreement with the service. Medical transcription services are not covered entities. So, in this arrangement, you are a subcontractor and would only need to comply with the subcontractor agreement you sign with the service. However, the medical transcription service will promise their clients that their subcontractors (you) will protect private health information. You should expect a statement about this in your agreement with the service.

15. *As an independent contractor, would there ever be a situation for which I would need to sign more than one agreement with a client? Doesn't a business associate agreement cover everything?*

    A business associate agreement only covers Privacy Rule requirements. It does not cover topics such as how you will bill your client and how he or she will reimburse you for services. You can add language about the Privacy Rule into a regular contract for services, or you can have two separate agreements—one for your service and one for Privacy Rule requirements.

16. *Do I really need two computers in my home—one for my medical transcription work and one for my family?*

    No, not if you can secure protected health information on your computer, so that your family members cannot access it. This can be done with separate login information and separate passwords. It can also be done by creating two partitions on the hard drive of your computer, so that your transcription work is on one partition and only accessible by you. The family can then log on to the other partition for their use.

17. *I am what is called a remote employee, not an independent contractor, even though I work from my home office. Seems to me, I don't need to do anything about the Privacy Rule, except what my employee agreement requires. Correct?*

    That is correct. Your employer's policies will outline what you have to do to protect the information, whether you are an employee of a hospital (a covered entity) or a medical transcription service (a business associate).

18. *My client is a physician who only has offices in the hospital. Would the physician's privacy policies or the hospital's privacy policies affect me? Who would I sign my business associate agreement with—the physician or the hospital?*

    This depends on the physician's relationship with the hospital. Your agreements will be determined by whether he is simply a physician who rents space in the hospital or whether he is an employee of the hospital. In the first situation, your agreement would be with him. In the second, your agreement would be with the hospital. The physician's office should be able to tell you what is required.

19. *Should I initiate a business associate agreement if my client doesn't? Which of us would keep the original?*

    It is the responsibility of the covered entity (your client, in this case) to have a business associate agreement with all of their business associates. If they do not do this, it is suggested that you provide it yourself. By having an agreement ready to sign, you show you can provide a value-added service to your clients. In addition, it is generally a good idea to create two originals of any agreement and have both parties sign both copies, so that each person can keep an original.

20. *Our transcription service accidentally sent a report to the wrong physician. What steps do we need to take?*

    Your client needs to be informed of the breach. You should fill out a "report of disclosure" form and send it to your client. The transcription service should keep the form for six years. In addition, through your disciplinary procedure, you should address the incident with the employee or contractor responsible for the breach.

21. *A medical transcriptionist in our company made a simple mistake and sent a copy of a report to the wrong physician. Termination of her employment seems to be too severe. What other options might we have?*

There may be times when someone makes a simple mistake that causes a breach of privacy. Your policy on sanctions should address this. One option is to place a verbal warning in this employee's file that addresses what happened, why it was wrong, and that it should not happen in the future. The Privacy Rule does not require that an employee be terminated for breaching information. It does require that your sanctions policy show that you have addressed the issue.

22. *I provide medical transcription services for a physician who says he does not need to be concerned with HIPAA because he only deals with workmen's compensation and that it is exempt from HIPAA. Is this true?*

There are several insurances listed in the Privacy Rule that are exempt from its requirements. Workmen's compensation is in this category, as it is not considered a "health plan." However, the definition of a "healthcare provider" does fit your physician, and he should be compliant with the Privacy Rule. The exemption only applies to the workmen's compensation insurance program, not to the physician.

AAMT Paper on Special Considerations for Offsite Medical Transcriptionists

◉ INTRODUCTION

The transcription industry as a whole increasingly uses offsite medical transcriptionists, whether as employees, independent contractors, or business associates. Special consideration must be taken in this setting to ensure protection of the information. The 2004 AAMT Legislative Task Force created a checklist to be used with offsite medical transcriptionists, which is published here with permission of both AAMT and the authors.

SAFEGUARDING PROTECTED HEALTH INFORMATION (PHI): FOCUS POINTS FOR OFFSITE TRANSCRIPTIONISTS

by Diane J. Hatch and Renee M. Priest, CMT, Members of AAMT's 2004 Legislative Task Force

The HIPAA Privacy and Security rules hold the provider, referred to as the Covered Entity (CE), directly responsible for breaches of privacy and security, and the rules require the provider in turn to contractually obligate/hold responsible those business associates who assist them with the medical record documentation process. Because the rules were written with a "best practices" approach and do not specify particular software programs or methods of data transfer, and because the level of knowledge regarding HIPAA varies greatly among hospitals, large clinic groups, and smaller provider groups, there is a great deal of inconsistency in what CEs are asking their business associates to do. If you are a Medical Transcription Service Owner (MTSO) or an Independent Contractor (IC), you must become familiar with HIPAA Privacy and Security regulations as well as your state's privacy laws, as state laws will supersede HIPAA if they are more stringent. If you routinely process records of patients from other states, you must become aware of regulations in those states as well. If you are an employee, it is your employer, whether MTSO or institution, that bears the responsibility for ensuring that you are aware of regulations that may affect how you work and how you safeguard protected health information (PHI) in an offsite location. The use of PHI, as well as specific demographic data as mandated by insurance and other healthcare agencies, is an integral and necessary part of the documentation process. There are two main issues for medical transcriptionists (MTs): Use and disclosure of PHI by MTSO and MTs, and transfer of data between provider, MTSO and MTs.

USE AND DISCLOSURE.

The issue of privacy is one that MTs have been familiar with long before the HIPAA standards were written. Although MTs use PHI in the course of their work, they are almost never authorized to disclose it to anyone other than their MTSO or the client. The supposition is that all persons involved in the healthcare process in any capacity will always treat the information entrusted to them responsibly and ethically. All MTs should understand exactly what responsible and ethical means in this context and should be willing to sign a statement stating so.

TRANSFER OF DATA.

Transfer of data from the provider to an MT usually occurs in one of three different ways: the dictator speaks into a hand-held or desk dictation unit with removable tapes that are given to the MT; the dictator speaks into a phone-in recording system either at the institution or the transcription service, which the MT accesses by phoning into the same system; or the dictator speaks into a phone-in or hand-held digital recording system that transfers a voice file directly to the MT's computer. Transfer of data from the transcriptionist to the provider can also occur in several ways. Text files can be encrypted and e-mailed to the provider, printed by the transcriptionist and delivered after printing, printed remotely by the transcriptionist on the provider's printer, or transferred to the provider's location by direct PC-to-PC connection or over the Internet. The safest and most practical way to accomplish these transfers between providers and offsite MTs is to have the MT work on a computer provided by the institution or transcription company in an enclosed home office setting, with the computer set up in such a way that prevents the MT from printing, copying, or in any other manner saving or retaining either the report, the voice file, or any of the patient demographics that were pulled into the report. The institution or company then assumes all responsibility for hardware/software repair and maintenance, thus bypassing the need to remove PHI from hard drives before independent maintenance/repair is undertaken. As the company or institution owns the equipment, they can require the MT to refrain from installing any other software which may interfere with security precautions and to refrain from sharing the computer with family members. Some institutions allow use of Internet sites for terminology research, some do not. The MT should be provided with clear instructions regarding responsibilities for maintenance and updating of software/hardware. Although a CE is required to delineate specific privacy and security requirements in his or her contracts with business associates, we feel there should also be a minimum standard of Privacy and Security precautions that every offsite medical transcriptionist, whether independent contractor, employee, or MTSO, should follow. Because HIPAA uses the terms "scalability" and "reasonable," many of the items listed below are not specifically required by the regulations but are instead AAMT's recommendations for best practices to protect a patient's health information. These are intended to provide a foundation upon which more restrictive client-specific requirements can be built.

OFFSITE CHECKLIST.

Confidentiality Agreement. All MTs, whether IC or employee, should be required to sign a confidentiality agreement stating that disclosure of confidential information to anyone other than the client or MTSO is prohibited. Disclosure of confidential information is prohibited indefinitely, even after termination of the contract or business agreement. Confidentiality requirements do not end when the business relationship ends. All MTs should be expected to uphold the Code of Ethics adopted by the American Association for Medical Transcription with regard to PHI.

Documentation of Training. All MTs, whether IC or employee, should have documentation of having received appropriate training, either in HIPAA and state regulations involving security and privacy of PHI or in the institution or transcription company's policies and procedures regarding safeguarding PHI.

Work Performed in a Secure Area. The offsite MT should provide documentation to certify that work will be performed in a secure area, in either an office with a door that can be locked or an area that is accessed only by the MT with the computer facing away from view by passersby and that appropriate safeguards are taken to prevent anyone overhearing the voice files while processing reports.

Destruction of Hard Copy PHI. Shredders should be used for printed material containing PHI such as patient appointment or hospital census sheets. If faxes are received on a machine that uses roll-style film cartridges to print, these need to be destroyed as they preserve a complete copy of any faxed material.

OTHER MEDIA.

- Physical Media: Information sent via audiocassette or other media (disks) that needs to be shipped or mailed should have a designated recipient who must sign upon receipt and should only be sent by a carrier who can track the shipment. When not in use, such media should be stored in a locked, fireproof receptacle/storage cabinet.
- Faxing: If faxes are sent by the MT, transmittal confirmation sheets should be saved for future verification. The MT should always use a fax cover sheet. Preprogrammed fax numbers should be used whenever

possible, and when not preprogrammed, the number dialed should be verified before hitting "send."

- E-Mail: Encryption of e-mail and attachments containing PHI is recommended. The Security Rule designates this as an "addressable" issue, meaning that it is up to the Covered Entity to decide whether to encrypt and to what level.

Access to Voice Files and Demographic Databases. Passwords should be required for access. The offsite MT is responsible for maintaining confidentiality by never sharing passwords or access and always logging out of databases or transcription platform when finished. Each person is accountable for all activity under his or her password and account.

Offsite Computer Security. If transcription is done on a company- or institution-owned computer, the owner of the computer should be responsible for securing it (see above). If transcription is done on an MT-owned computer:

A. The MT must provide the employer or client with a signed statement assuring that the computer used to process PHI is a work tool and is not shared by other family members. If this is not possible for some reason, the MT must provide assurance that acceptable measures have been taken to ensure patient confidentiality, such as password protected folders and encrypted files. Passwords must be kept secure and should be changed frequently (also see Disaster Recovery section below). A password-protected screen saver and the habit of locking the computer whenever one steps away from it is also recommended.

B. The MT should have a basic working knowledge of the hardware/software programs used.

C. Computers with Internet access should have active firewalls in place to prevent others from gaining access to the computer without the MT's knowledge.

D. Anti-virus programs, operating systems (i.e., Windows® updates) and spyware detection software should be kept up to date with periodic upgrades as recommended by the manufacturer.

E. Many kinds of software contain "automatic update" capabilities that enable them to update themselves by connecting to an internet site to download and install new things automatically, potentially allowing unauthorized access to files kept in the computers. The update capability should be turned off and should be performed manually when necessary.

F. Software programs such as games and music programs that allow file sharing should not be installed on any computer where PHI is used.

G. Work should be returned immediately upon completion and no copy should be stored on the hard drive. When PHI is retained until the client/service acknowledges receipt and payment is received, then it should be removed from the computer, transferred to disk/CD, and stored securely in a fireproof, locked cabinet or receptacle. Once receipt is acknowledged and payment received, the media should then be appropriately destroyed. Work logs should be handled in the same manner.

H. If computer equipment must be repaired, all PHI should be removed from the computer hard drive. If a hard drive is replaced, the MT should ensure that the old hard drive is destroyed. A record should be kept of who made the repairs.

Disaster Recovery/Backup Planning. Precautions should be taken for equipment failure and adverse environmental conditions such as power outages.

A. Set software applications that have auto backup features to a frequency of 2 to 5 minutes.

B. Use surge protectors for computers and other devices such as transcribers, including both electrical connections and phone line connections.

C. Consider a UPS backup power supply for computers, so that MTs will have a few minutes to save documents in the event of a power outage.

D. Back up text files to a removable backup device (floppy, CD, etc.) on a daily basis in case work needs to be re-sent and the computer is down.

E. Routinely back up any voice files that have not been transcribed to a second computer or removable media in case of computer failure.

F. If a digital dictation system is used, consider developing an alternate method of dictation (i.e., hand-held recorders) for use if the system is down.

G. Develop an alternate method for returning work if the normal manner is not available, such as if Internet access is unavailable.

H. The offsite MT's employer or MTSO should always have updated computer passwords in case the MT is incapacitated. The MT should also provide an emergency contact person who can physically access the MT's work area and computer. In an emergency, the employer or MTSO can give the emergency contact the passwords and have any PHI retained by the MT retrieved or destroyed. If tapes are used, the emergency contact person should be aware of where untyped tapes are kept so that these can be returned to the employer or MTSO immediately. In the event of the MT's death or permanent disability, sending the computer to the employer or MTSO for removal of PHI is recommended.

Contract Termination. Upon termination, the MT will provide certification that all PHI and demographic information has been appropriately returned and/or destroyed.

Security/Privacy Breach. In the case of unauthorized disclosure or theft of PHI or hardware, the employer, medical transcription company or client must be notified immediately. Steps must be taken to ensure that further breaches will not occur and these steps must be documented for the CE.

References:
"AHIMA Practice Brief: Facsimile Transmission of Health Information":
http://library.ahima.org/xpedio/groups/public/documents/ahima/pub_bok2_000116.html

"Final Privacy Rule," as published in the *Federal Register,* August 14, 2002:
http://www.hhs.gov/ocr/hipaa/privrulepd.pdf

Office of Civil Rights—HIPAA Assistance:
http://www.hhs.gov/ocr/hipaa/assist.html

Office of Civil Rights—Privacy Questions & Answers:
http://answers.hhs.gov/cgi-bin/hhs.cfg/php/enduser/std_alp.php

Industry Resources

GOVERNMENT SITES

Centers for Medicare and Medicaid Services (CMS)
www.cms.hhs.gov

CMS is the organization responsible for all rules except the Privacy Rule. You can find on the CMS website updated information related to compliance to all other HIPAA rules.

Final Privacy Rule Text
www.hhs.gov/ocr/hipaa/finalreg.html

This site offers the final actual text of the Privacy Rule in a variety of downloadable formats. You can choose the one that fits your computer system best.

National Committee on Vital and Health Statistics (NCVHS)
www.ncvhs.dhhs.gov

NCVHS is an advisor to the Secretary of the U.S. Department of Health and Human Resources. NCVHS holds hearings to gather information about the impact of the rules on the workplace. Following hearings, this group formulates recommendations and shares them with the Secretary, who will consider including them in future rules.

Office of Civil Rights
www.hss.gov/ocr/hipaa

The Office of Civil Rights has a website for all HIPAA-related issues. The frequently-asked-questions section of the site addresses many concerns about compliance with the Privacy Rule. It also provides links for filing complaints with the Office of Civil Rights.

U.S. Department of Health and Human Services, Administrative Simplification
aspe.hhs.gov/admnsimp/index.shtml

If you want HIPAA-related information right from the original source, you will find it on this web page entitled "Administrative Simplification in the Health Care Industry." It offers downloadable PDF files on many topics related to HIPAA and includes links to other HIPAA-related sites.

U.S. Government Printing Office
www.gpoaccess.gov

The U.S. Government Printing Office is the place to contact if you want to order copies of the *Federal Register* or any other government publication.

 ## PROFESSIONAL ASSOCIATIONS AND STANDARDS ORGANIZATIONS

American Association for Medical Transcription
www.aamt.org

The American Association for Medical Transcription (AAMT) has been the professional organization representing medical transcriptionists since 1978. AAMT sets standards of practice and education for medical transcriptionists, administers a certification program, has established a code of ethics, and advocates on behalf of the profession. There are over 135 component associations of AAMT, each of which holds regular educational meetings and symposia. Address: 100 Sycamore Avenue, Modesto, CA 95354. Telephone: 800-982-2182.

American Health Information Management Association
www.ahima.org

The American Health Information Management Association (AHIMA) is a professional association whose members work in a variety of care settings including hospitals, physician offices, managed care organizations, and long-term care facilities. AHIMA is very active in shaping industry standards, legislation, regulation, education government agencies, and the public about health information management issues. Address: 233 North Michigan Avenue, Suite 2150, Chicago, IL 60601-5519. Telephone: 312-233-1100.

American Medical Informatics Association
www.amia.org

The American Medical Informatics Association (AMIA) includes members who are dedicated to the development and application of information technology that supports patient care, teaching, research, and health-care administrators. Address: 4915 St. Elmo Avenue, Suite 401, Bethesda, MD 20814. Telephone: 301-657-1291.

American National Standards Institute
www.ansi.org

The American National Standards Institute (ANSI) is a private, nonprofit organization [501(c)3] that administers and co-ordinates the U.S. voluntary standardization and conformity assessment system. Its mission is to enhance both the global competitiveness of U.S. business and the U.S. quality of life by promoting and facilitating voluntary consensus standards and conformity assessment systems, and safeguarding their integrity. Address: 1819 L Street NW, Washington, DC 20036. Telephone: 202-293-8020.

American Society for Testing and Materials (ASTM) www.astm.org

ASTM (they prefer to not use their expanded name) is a standards development organization. Within ASTM's committee on the electronic health record is a subcommittee on medical transcription. Address: 100 Barr Harbor Drive, West Conshohocken, PA 19428-2959. Telephone: 610-832-9585.

Center for Healthcare Information Management www.chim.org

The Center for Healthcare Information Management (CHIM) is driving the adoption of strategic information management and technology in the health industry. CHIM members seek to bring a greater awareness and understanding among healthcare professionals on how information technology can be harnessed to improve the quality and cost effectiveness of health care. Address: 3800 Packard Road, Suite 150, Ann Arbor, MI 48108. Telephone: 734-937-6116.

Healthcare Information and Management Systems Society www.himss.org

The Healthcare Information and Management Systems Society (HIMSS) is an organization whose members are primarily the information technology workers in the healthcare industry. They are actively involved preparing for the future of the electronic health record. Address: 230 East Ohio Street, Suite 500, Chicago, IL 60611-3269. Telephone: 312-664-HIMSS.

OTHER RESOURCES

Alan Goldberg's Law, Technology, and Change Homepage www.healthlawyer.com

Alan Goldberg is a past president of the American Health Lawyers Association. He is a nationally recognized speaker on HIPAA and the Privacy Rule. His website offers valuable information for those wishing to know and understand HIPAA, as well as other legal issues in health care.

Health Privacy Project
www.healthprivacy.org

This is an organization based at Georgetown University in Washington, D.C. Their primary focus is privacy issues in health care. Their website offers great HIPAA resources, as well as a link for researching state privacy laws related to the health-care industry.

Workgroup for Electronic Data Interchange
www.wedi.org

The Workgroup for Electronic Data Interchange (WEDI) is the organization that provides advisories to the Secretary of the U.S. Department of Health and Human Services on how proposed regulations will impact the industry as a whole. WEDI has been very active in the creation and implementation of the rules. Address: 12020 Sunrise Valley Dr., Suite 100, Reston, VA 20191. Telephone: 703-391-2716.

RESOURCES FOR TRAINING

Training sessions for medical transcriptionists related to the HIPAA Privacy Rule can often be found at AAMT meetings, either on a national, state, or local level. For more information, visit the AAMT website at www.aamt.org.

Glossary

Medical transcriptionists have an insatiable thirst for knowing what acronyms and abbreviations stand for. This glossary includes some of the more common ones related to the Privacy Rule. While not all of the entries may be found in this book, you will want to be familiar with them all as you delve into the world of health care in general and the Privacy Rule in specific.

AAMT: American Association for Medical Transcription.

Administrative Simplification Subtitle: portion of the HIPAA legislation that includes the Privacy Rule, created because studies showed that simplifying how information is processed would reduce costs in health care. *Also referred to as* Administrative Simplification Subsection of the HIPAA legislation.

AHIMA: American Health Information Management Association.

AMIA: American Medical Informatics Association.

ANSI: American National Standards Institute.

ASTM: American Society for Testing and Materials. The group prefers to go by ASTM.

business associate: an individual or entity who is not a part of the workforce but who performs a function for a covered entity using protected health information.

business associate agreement: a contract that outlines the duties and responsibilities of a business associate in his or her dealings with a covered entity. *Also referred to as* business associate contract.

CE: covered entity.

Centers for Medicare and Medicaid Services (CMS): the agency responsible for enforcement of all of the HIPAA rules except the Privacy Rule.

CHIM: Center for Healthcare Information Management.

CMS: Centers for Medicare and Medicaid Services. *Formerly called* the Health Care Finance Administration (HCFA).

confidentiality agreement: the agreement that is signed to guarantee the confidentiality of a patient's records.

contract for services: the contract between a medical transcription service or independent contractor and the client. It outlines services provided and methods of payment.

covered entity: the group ultimately accountable for adherence to the Privacy Rule, which includes health plans, healthcare clearinghouses, and healthcare providers.

de-identified information: information that has been stripped of all identifying details about a patient, such that there is no reasonable belief that it can be used to identify the individual. A covered entity must have someone with appropriate knowledge and experience with statistical and scientific principles evaluate this, documenting both the methods used and the results of analysis.

DHHS: U.S. Department of Health and Human Services.

disclosure: sharing information outside the covered entity's control, which requires authorization from the patient.

DSMO: designated standard maintenance organization.

EHR: electronic health record.

EMR: electronic medical record.

health care: services or supplies related to the health of an individual.

health information: any information related to someone's past, present, or future mental or physical health or to past, present, or future payment for health care.

health plan: an insurance company or any program or plan that provides for payment of the cost of health care.

healthcare clearinghouse: a group that processes protected health information for others, usually changing its language or format to standard ones.

healthcare operations: activities that are required for a covered entity to conduct business, such as peer reviews, quality assurance activities, and medical transcription.

healthcare provider: a physician and/or healthcare facility.

HHS: U.S. Department of Health and Human Services. Also *DHHS*.

HIMSS: Healthcare Information and Management Systems Society.

HIPAA: Health Insurance Portability and Accountability Act of 1996. This is the legislation, of which the Privacy Rule is a part. *Also referred to as* Public Law 104-191.

IC: independent contractor.

independent contractor: a self-employed person who provides services to others; a medical transcriptionist who is an independent contractor may be classified as either a business associate or a subcontractor.

ISO: International Standards Organization.

JCAHO: Joint Commission for Accreditation of Hospital Organizations.

MT: medical transcriptionist.

MTSO: medical transcription service owner.

Notice of Privacy Practices: a document provided to patients that tells how their health information will be used and protected.

NPRM: notice of proposed rule making.

OCR: Office of Civil Rights.

Office of Civil Rights (OCR): the agency responsible for enforcement of the HIPAA Privacy Rule. It is a part of the U.S. Department of Health and Human Services.

PHI: protected health information.

privacy officer: the person responsible for the privacy program for a covered entity; a position required by the Privacy Rule.

protected health information: health information that contains data that can reasonably identify the patient.

SDO: standards development organization.

Secretary: the Secretary of Health and Human Services or any other officer or employee of the U. S. Department of Health and Human Services to whom the authority involved has been delegated.

SSO: standards setting organization.

standard setting organization (SSO): an organization accredited by the American National Standards Institute (ANSI) that develops and maintains standards for information transactions and data elements. *Also referred to as a* standards development organization.

standard: a condition or requirement that describes specific criteria for products, systems, services, or practices related to the privacy of individually identifiable health information; classification of components. May include specification of materials, performance, or operations, or delineation of procedures.

state preemption: refers to state law having precedence over the Privacy Rule. This occurs when state law gives a patient more protection than the rule does.

subcontractor: a self-employed person who provides services to the person or entity who holds the client contract. A medical transcriptionist who is a subcontractor provides services to a business associate.

use: sharing health information within an entity, which requires no authorization from the patient.

VPN: Virtual Private Network.

WEDI: Workgroup for Electronic Data Interchange.

workforce: employees and paid or unpaid volunteers, trainees, and other personnel whose conduct in the performance of work for a covered entity is under the direct control of that entity. Independent contractors are not considered part of a workforce.

Workgroup for Electronic Data Interchange (WEDI): an advisory group to the U.S. Department of Health and Human Services. WEDI makes recommendations about upcoming rules and procedures, as well as develop standards in the healthcare industry.